PICTURE MAP GEOGRAPHY OF THE USSR

by Alexander Nazaroff

Published by J. B. Lippincott Company

The reviewers say:

"Written by a well-known authority on Russia, this
geography first presents a brief overview of the
lands and peoples of the Soviet Union, Russian history, and the physical features of the land, natural
resources, vegetation, climate, major cities, and
industrial areas. Similar in format to others in
the series, the text is compact, unbiased, and amply
detailed; clear pen-and-ink maps show representative
landmarks and local products. . .useful well-indexed
reference source. . ."

---Library Journal

Other Picture Map Geographies

PICTURE MAP GEOGRAPHY OF THE USSR

⋙ ★ ⋘

Alexander Nazaroff

Illustrated by Thomas R. Funderburk

J. B. Lippincott Company

PHILADELPHIA AND NEW YORK

★

CONTENTS

Picture Map Geography of
THE USSR

I

★

COUNTRY, PEOPLE,
HISTORY, ORGANIZATION

Russia's official name is now the Union of Soviet Socialist Republics, or, briefly, the Soviet Union. The largest country in the world with a continuous, unbroken territory, it sprawls over two continents—the eastern half of Europe and the northern third of Asia. It occupies *one-sixth* of the entire land surface of our globe and is more than two and a half times as large as the United States, seven times the size of India, and ninety times that of the Federal Republic of Germany. When midnight strikes in Moscow it is 10 A.M. at Cape Dezhnev, Russia's easternmost point.

The total length of the Soviet Union's frontier is one and a half times that of the equator. Two-thirds of it is formed by oceans—the Arctic and the Pacific—and by a number of seas. The remaining one-third extends overland. The great bulk of the Soviet Union's territory is an immense plain.

The dividing line between Europe and Asia is the long, low range of Ural Mountains running north to south. Asiatic Russia east of the Urals, with the exception of a narrow strip along the Pacific, is called Siberia. Here and there the great Russian plain rises gently, giving way to uplands, but then slopes down again. In Eastern Siberia, however, uplands pass into mountain ranges. Most of Asiatic Russia's southern border is very rugged. Here some of the world's loftiest snow mountains shoulder themselves high into the sky and glaciers descend from them into the valleys. Such are the Tyan-Shan and the Pamir-Alay ranges and the windswept Pamir Plateau, called "the roof of the world." High, too—higher than the Swiss Alps—are the Caucasian Mountains between the Black and the Caspian seas.

That structure of the country greatly affects its climate. Warm winds from the Baltic and the Mediterranean areas soften much of European Russia's climate. Winter and summer temperature in the Moscow area is similar to that of southern Canada. But mountains framing Asiatic Russia from the east and southeast shut off the moderating winds from the Pacific and most of Siberia, especially Eastern Siberia, is extremely cold—much colder than regions lying at the same latitude in European Russia.

Although the European part of the Soviet Union is only one-third the size of its Asiatic part, it is much more important.

It was in the western regions of European Russia that Russian history began in the ninth century. From there the Russians gradually expanded eastward—much as the Americans expanded westward from the Atlantic shore. A great majority of Russia's population still lives in European Russia and this is the location for the great Russian cities, such as Moscow, Leningrad, and Kiev or Kharkov, the bulk of the country's agriculture and manufacturing industries, most of its railways, its main intellectual centers, leading universities and theaters. Of course industrialization and modern civilization also penetrate eastward. In Siberia's virgin forests new cities are springing up and important new industrial areas are appearing. But the development of a land as huge as Asiatic Russia takes time.

In climate, nature, and type of life, the Soviet Union may be subdivided from north to south into the following main zones or belts.

The tundra zone is washed by the Arctic Ocean and its seas. These are desolate lands of ice, cold, and swampy tundra; of the Arctic winter night lasting for months; of the reindeer, the walrus, and the polar bear. In summer, millions of birds flock there to regale themselves on fish. The population, made up largely of some small Finno-Ugric tribes, of Nentsy (Samoyeds), and the slant-eyed Yakuts, is scant. Settlements of fishermen or trappers are few. Only in the west of the zone are there large centers such as the ports of Archangel and Murmansk with their large fishing fleets.

The forest belt is very wide, occupying more than half of Russia's entire territory. The northern part of European Russia remains rich in great coniferous woods. In the rest of it—especially in the industrial areas of Moscow, Ivanovo, Gorky—forests have largely given place to plowlands, cities, and villages, with industrial developments. The whole of Siberia, however, except for its agricultural southwestern sector, is still one continuous, immense, forbidding forest. Most of it is pine, spruce, fir, larch, and cedar (with a fringe of deciduous woods in the south of the belt). The Russians call it *taiga*. The *taiga* is inhabited by the wolf, the brown bear, the fox, the elk, the valuable sable—and by only few human beings. Long winters are very severe here, summers short and hot. Large cities and civilization cling chiefly to the Trans-Siberian Railroad which runs all along Siberia's southern rim, from the Pacific shore to Moscow. There are, of course, some developments even in the far north—timber and mining industry. Siberia is extremely rich in all natural resources, from coal, gold, oil, and diamonds to iron, copper, uranium, and numberless other ores. But access to them, except by plane, is often very difficult.

South of Kiev, Kazan, and Novosibirsk, the forests thin out. The intermediary *wooded steppe belt* begins, in which prairies are dotted with groves, especially in ravines and along rivers. It varies in width. Eventually, it is superseded by the pure *steppe belt*, which runs down to the shores of the Black Sea, includes the Northern Caucasus and a wide region along the Volga River, and passes into Southwestern Siberia.

Both these belts are important industrial areas. But primarily they are "Russia's granary," her great agricultural and cattle breeding zone. The endless, undulating fields of wheat remind one of our Middle West. In the western part of the zone, called the Ukraine, are sunlit villages, often sitting near a pond with weeping willows by it. The Ukrainian peasants' white stucco cabins with thatched roofs are surrounded with sunflowers and orchards. Winters are mild and the population is dense.

South of Western Siberia lies Kazakhstan (also very rich in natural resources) and other countries of the Soviet Central Asia.

In that vast region, steppes gradually pass into *the semi-desert and desert belt*. Large areas of it are real, waterless, sandy desert, characterized by intense dry heat in the summer; violent sandstorms blinding man and beast alike; and camel caravans. The desert is rich in reptiles—snakes, including the deadly cobra, and lizards as long as five feet. In the reeds near the few rivers are occasional tigers.

Nearby rise the great Tyan-Shan ranges and the Pamir Plateau. Their foothill valleys are very fertile. Wherever adequately watered by nature or man, they produce bumper crops of cotton, wheat, rice, and delicious fruit. Here the population, chiefly of Kazakhs, Uzbeks, Kirgizes, and other Turkic peoples, is quite dense. In their Oriental dress—long, robelike *khalats* and wide fur caps, or small embroidered ones—these men look picturesque. Some of them are nomadic cattle-breeders living in felt tents, chiefly in mountain areas. In bygone centuries these lands played quite a role in the Mohammedan world and remarkable ancient cities can still be found. Samarkand, for example, dates back to the fourth century B.C.

Finally, the Soviet Union also has some isolated *subtropical areas* which lie along the country's southern border, in regions sheltered from cold winds by mountains. One is the shore of the Crimean Peninsula on the warm Black Sea. Another is the Transcaucasian (South Caucasian) shore of that sea from Sochi to Batumi.

In the latter area grow palms, tangerines, oranges, bamboos, eucalyptus, and cascades of flowers. Both regions, especially the sunny Crimea, may be called the Soviet Union's playground, a sort of Russian Florida.

In October, while people are still going in for a swim and sunning themselves on the sand at Yalta in the Crimea, somewhere in Sredne-Kolymsk in Eastern Siberia the temperature may well sink to −25° F.

In population the Soviet Union holds the third place in the world, after continental China and India. In 1966 there were 232,000,000 inhabitants. It is a multinational country, with over sixty languages spoken in it.

Over three-quarters of these people are Russians in the wider sense of the word. The Russians belong to the Slavic group of peoples. It is a large group, the same as the Germanic group, the Turkic group, or the Latins. There are Western Slavs, such as the Poles or the Czechs, Southern Slavs—Serbians or Bulgarians—and Eastern Slavs, or Russians. The Russians, in turn, are subdivided into three main branches: the "Great" Russians, or Russians proper, the Ukrainians, and the Belorussians (or White Russians). The Great Russians are by far the most numerous; they form 55 percent of the Soviet Union's entire population. Though each of these branches speaks a distinct language of its own, the languages have a great deal in common. A Russian easily understands a Ukrainian or a Belorussian.

But the remaining 57,500,000 inhabitants of the Soviet Union belong to various non-Russian nationalities. Some 13,500,000 are various peoples of the Turkic group. Such are the Kazan Tartars, the Bashkirs, and the Chuvashes, in the eastern part of European Russia; the Kazakhs, Uzbeks, Turkmens, and Kirghizes in Central Asia; and the Yakuts, the Abakan Tartars, and other people in Siberia. Some of these peoples are descended from the Tartars who, centuries ago, invaded and long dominated European Russia. Among the Soviet Union's non-Russian nationalities there are also those of the Finno-Ugric group, scattered chiefly in the north and east of European Russia. Among them are the Finns proper, the Esthonians, the Karelians, and the Mordovians. As a rule they are solidly built, blond, and of medium height.

There are in the Soviet Union about 3 million Jews. Russia has also some Mongolians, such as the Kalmyks, along the lower Volga, and the Buryats in Eastern Siberia. In Transcaucasia, besides other nationalities, live about 2,900,000 Armenians and 3,000,000 Georgians. Both possess a highly developed and very old Christian culture of their own. In the mountain valleys of the Northern Caucasus is a crazy quilt of tiny peoples, such as the Tats, the Adygheys, and the Kabardinians. They count anywhere from 3,700 to 260,000 men each; yet each has a language and a distinct "ethnic personality" of its own. Most of these mountaineers are colorful. They are excellent riders, proud, wild-tempered, quick with the dagger, but true and faithful friends. To these nationalities mentioned, many more might be added.

When and how did that immense, multinational country come into being?

Nestor, a pious monk of Kiev and author of the earliest Russian Chronicle (or history), gives the following account of its origin.

In the ninth century of our era, he writes, the tribes of Eastern Slavs which lived in the country between the slopes of the Carpathian Mountains and the Dnieper River felt that they could not govern themselves well, for they were continually quarreling. Messengers were sent "beyond the sea" to the warlike Scandinavian people called *Rus*, with which they had fought before. These messengers said to their former enemies: "Our land is large and plentiful, but it lacks order. Come over, then, to be our masters and rulers."

The chieftain of the Rus, named Ryurik (or Hroerekr), accepted the invitation. He established himself with his kin and warriors in the Slav city of Novgorod. His descendants intermarried with the Slavs and spoke their tongue. They became the Eastern Slavs' hereditary rulers and united their tribes into a state. The younger of Ryurik's descendants were called princes and ruled over local principalities. Their grand duke reigned over them in Kiev, which became the first capital of the new country. The Eastern Slavs took over the name of their new rulers' original nationality. They began to call their land and themselves *Rus,* and eventually *Russia* and *Russians.*

Thus, according to Nestor, "Russia came to be." Originally, the Russians were one people. The first signs of their division into Great Russians, Ukrainians, and White Russians began to appear only in the twelfth to fourteenth centuries.

In the beginning, the new State held just the basins of some rivers. The Russians had no written language, lived in mud hovels or primi-

tive log cabins, and wore skins. However, the country developed rapidly. In 988 the Russians adopted Christianity. The religion had been brought to them by Greek monks from Constantinople, capital of the Eastern Empire, with which they carried on a thriving trade. What had been wilderness gave way to plowlands. Kiev became a lovely city with magnificent churches. In provincial principalities appeared new cities with fortress walls of wood.

But the new nation faced an extremely hard struggle for national survival. Russia constantly suffered invasions from nomadic peoples, mostly Turkic. Disgorged by Asia, these nomads swept westward, through the southern steppe belt. This was an ideal avenue for invasions, with plenty of grass for the nomads' cattle and horses. The invaders yearly raided, sacked, and burned Kievan Russia's cities. At the same time, the Russians repeatedly fought in the northwest, trying to ward off the heavily pressing Germans and Swedes.

Later, the mighty, mounted Mongolian-Tartar hordes appeared out of Mongolia. In 1240, led by the redoubtable Kahn Batu, they conquered Russia in a series of bloody battles. The heavy Tartar Yoke lasted for 240 years and looked as though it would be Russia's end. But internal dissent eventually weakened the Golden Horde, or Mongolian-Tartar State on the lower Volga River. Aided by this discord and by other factors, the Russians shook off the yoke.

They themselves advanced against the Tartars as the latter retreated into Asia. In 1582, largely through sheer luck, the Russians seized the Khanate (Kingdom) of Siberia east of the Urals—a khanate which soon lent its name to the whole huge country. Within the next sixty years the Russians dominated most of Siberia and emerged, in 1648, on the Pacific shore. Most of this land had been won by Russian pioneers and by Russian trappers in quest of furs, rather than by soldiers.

While migrating north and advancing east after the retreating Tartars, the Russians came in close contact with scattered Finno-Ugric tribes who had always lived in Russia's forest belt. The Russians intermingled with some of them, fought with others, and bypassed yet other ones. Eventually they learned to live peacefully side by side with these neighbors. Such Finno-Ugric (and other) ethnical "islands" remain in the surrounding mass of Russians to this day.

In the thirteenth century the center of Russia's national life had shifted from Kiev to Central European Russia. Soon Moscow became the country's new capital. The grand dukes gradually took over all of the local principalities and became mighty rulers of the united Russian land. The princes became their leading nobles. The concentration of power in the hands of one man undoubtedly had helped Russia to shake off the Tartars. In 1547, under the astute, talented, but cruel Ivan IV—"The Terrible"—the grand dukes began to style themselves "tsars" and "autocrats." For after the conquest of the Eastern Empire (Constantinople) by the Turks in 1453, the Muscovite grand dukes regarded themselves as "spiritual heirs" of Eastern emperors, or autocrats. The authority of the Russian tsars was unlimited, absolute, "by the will of God."

In 1598 the Ryurik dynasty became extinct. After years of anarchy and civil wars, a new dynasty—the Romanovs—was elected to Muscovy's throne.

During the centuries of the Tartar Yoke, the Russians lived drawn into the Asiatic world, virtually isolated from Western Europe; they fell some two centuries behind the peoples of the West in their cultural development.

One of the tsars of the Romanov dynasty, Peter the Great (1682–1725), grasped this fact. He was a giant, standing six-foot-nine, and a genius as well. He carried out drastic reforms in order to Europeanize his subjects—to introduce them to Western ways of life, outlook, education, and science. After a long war with Sweden—then one of the strongest European powers—Peter wrested from it a wide belt of territory along the Baltic Sea. This included Finland, Estonia, Latvia, and Lithuania. Russia's emergence on the Baltic Sea greatly facilitated her trade and cultural contacts with the West.

All of these changes brought about by Peter greatly enhanced Russia's national and cultural development. In the nineteenth century the Russian people produced their first scientists, thinkers, writers.

Since Peter's time Russia's rulers were called emperors, and its capital was transferred to St. Petersburg (now Leningrad), a new city built on the Baltic shore. Under Peter's successors the splendor and magnificance of the Imperial Russian Court became renowned all over the world.

In our time, Russia's history has taken an entirely new turn. Few of Peter the Great's successors in the eighteenth and nineteenth centuries continued his reforms with anything like his farsightedness and energy. By the beginning of the twentieth century some of the old and serious ills of Russian life, instead of being cured, became worse.

In particular, among Russia's peasants (and peasants formed the majority of the population), many lacked land. They lived in poverty, coveting the noblemen's landed estates. Russian intellectual and business circles resented the lack of political freedom and wanted a greater share in the running of the nation's affairs, for the Emperor's authority still remained virtually autocratic. Despite Russia's wealth in natural resources, it was industrially backward compared to Western nations. This accounted for Russia's extremely heavy losses in human lives during World War I (1914–1919). Meanwhile, the last of the Emperors—Nicholas II—and most of his ministers lacked vision or determination to carry out necessary changes swiftly.

Therefore, in 1917—while World War I still raged—the Revolution broke out. That Revolution had nothing in common with the American Revolution. In this country Revolution was the birth of a nation. In Russia, it was a violent overthrow of the entire political, economic, and social order.

The centuries-old autocracy was swept away. A violent struggle among various parties and groups of population ensued. There was a long period of anarchy, mass executions, famines, embittered civil wars, and "foreign intervention." Rivers of blood were shed.

By 1921, however, it was the Bolshevik—or Communist—Party, led by Vladimir Lenin, that came out on top. Its victory was won by sheer force. As a vote taken in 1917 had shown, the majority of the population did not support it.

Since then, the Communist Party itself has undergone various changes, some accompanied by bloodshed. But it continues to rule over Russia and has established a new order in the country. It is the Communists who have set up the Union of Soviet Socialist Republics, as it stands today. They also dispossessed and annihilated, often with great ruthlessness, Russia's former monied classes—noblemen, businessmen, well-off peasants—and established Socialism.

Socialism, in its Soviet form, is an economic system under which one can own personal property—money, clothes, furniture, television sets, cars, even houses—provided no profit is derived from them. But one cannot own stores, factories, industrial plants, mines, railroads, or land. All such profit-yielding means of production belong to the entire people, that is to say, to the State. Thus, all business concerns in the Soviet Union are run by the Government.

Communists hold that such a system eliminates "the exploitation of man by man, of laborers by capitalists," and works for general prosperity and happiness. Most people in the Western World hold, to the contrary, that the Western system of free competitive enterprise and private property yields far better results. For it stimulates man's free creative initiative, instead of killing it by bureaucratic red tape, as does the Soviet system. Indeed, there is no denying that at present an average American, German, or Frenchman lives much better than an average Soviet citizen.

Are the Russians happy under Socialism? We don't know. They cannot express their real feelings. They have a Supreme Soviet—that is, Parliament, or Congress—elected by universal suffrage, which makes laws. Yet there is but one political party—the ruling Communist Party—in the country, and no other party has been allowed to exist. Hence, the Russians have no choice: at the elections they can vote only for Communists. Soviet citizens are allowed to criticize various particular aspects of Socialism, or the ways of its application, but not its fundamental principles. For Socialism is incorporated into the Soviet Constitution, and no one can safely raise a voice against it.

However, the Soviet rulers have greatly industrialized Russia, spurring on her economic development. Until recently, the mighty Soviet industries produced chiefly various machines, armaments, heavy equipment for steel mills, hydroelectric power plants or oil and gas industries, and not consumer goods needed in everyday life. Now, however, the Soviet Government is trying to satisfy the Soviet citizens' desires for a more comfortable life.

Soviet scientists have distinguished themselves in various fields of knowledge. In particular, they have made great contributions to nuclear physics, to the investigation of outer space, to medical science. Generally speaking, the Soviet Union is today one of the leading countries of the world. As for the Russian people, gradually, often imperceptibly, they are adjusting Socialism to their own requirements and tastes.

According to the Soviet Constitution, all nationalities within the Soviet Union are equal and enjoy the same rights. The larger of these nationalities have been constituted into "sovereign and independent Socialist Soviet Republics." The union of these republics—that is, the Soviet Union—was "freely entered into" by them in 1922. At present there are fifteen such Union Republics: among them are the Russian Soviet Federated Socialist Republic, Russia proper, or RSFSR; the Ukrainian Soviet Socialist Republic, or USSR; the Estonian SSR; the Georgian SSR; the Kazakh SSR; the Uzbek SSR. Each of the SSR's comprised in the Soviet Union borders also on some foreign State or States.

In theory, every Union Republic is a Sovereign State with its own constitution, flag, and council of ministers. It elects its representatives both to the Supreme Soviet in Moscow and to its own Supreme Soviet. It even has the right of seceding—that is, separating itself—from the Soviet Union, if it so desires.

In practice, however, all important matters are solved by the Soviet Union's Government in Moscow. In that Government the Russians, as the largest nationality, play by far the most important role. That Government runs the entire country's national affairs, such as national defense, foreign relations, declaration of war and conclusion of peace, basic principles of economic organization, and management of the main industries.

To the governments of the Union Republics belong criminal, civil, and social legislation (within the framework established by Moscow); the running of economic concerns of "republican importance" (some of the mines, plants, trade organizations), education, schools, universities, development of each given nationality's culture, theater, folklore, and literature. The development of national cultures is greatly encouraged by the Soviet Government—as long as the nationalities making up the Soviet Union remain true to the principles of Soviet Communism. Great events are made in Moscow of the visits and performances of the Georgian or Uzbek ballet or opera; Moscow publications devote much space to old manuscripts found in Armenia, or to a new novel by a Lithuanian writer. As for the "right of secession," most Western students of the Soviet Union doubt very much that any Union Republic would ever dare invoke it. The actual unity of all Union Republics is cemented from within by the Communist Party. For Soviet Communists, no matter whether they are Russian, Latvian, Armenian, or Kazakh, are held together by a close Communist unity.

Less economically developed or culturally advanced non-Russian nationalities also form units of their own, with their own government organizations, and are called *Autonomous* Soviet Socialist Republics, or ASSR's. There are twenty of these in four of the Union Republics, in Russia proper, Georgia, Azerbaidzhan, and Kazakhstan. The ASSR's greatly differ among themselves in size and population. The Kalmyk ASSR, for instance, numbers 241,000 inhabitants, while the Bashkir ASSR has a population of 3,719,000. Each ASSR is responsible, in the main matters of government, to the Union Republic of which it is a part. But in their local administrative, economic, and cultural affairs—including all stages of education—the ASSR's enjoy a wide autonomy.

Most autonomous republics—sixteen out of twenty—are in the Russian Republic. That makes it in itself a federation of nationalities. Therefore it is called not merely a Soviet Socialist Republic (SSR), but Soviet *Federated* Socialist Republic (SFSR). The RSFSR is by far the largest of all Union republics, both in territory and population. It occupies two-thirds of European Russia and all of Siberia.

The Soviet Constitution gives political recognition also to still smaller national groups, which could not support governments of their own. Such national groups form Autonomous Districts (AD's) or—still smaller ones—National Districts (ND's). There are eight AD's and ten ND's altogether in the Soviet Union. Their inhabitants can also have schools of their own and publish papers in their respective languages. These national units—the SSR's, the ASSR's, the AD's, the ND's—each send, according to its rank, an established number of representatives to the Soviet Nationalities, which is one of the two Chambers of the Supreme Soviet (an equivalent of our Congress) in Moscow.

Along with national divisions, all larger Union Republics also have purely administrative ones. They are divided into provinces which are mostly about as large as average autonomous republics. Such, for example, are the provinces of Moscow, Tula, and Saratov. If, however, there is within such an administrative division an Autonomous District (AD), that division is called a territory and not a province.

★

THE CENTRAL INDUSTRIAL REGION

 The Soviet Union's oldest and most important industrial region lies in the center of European Russia, around Moscow. It is about three-fourths the size of Texas. Besides the Province of Moscow there are eleven other provinces belonging to this region: Vladimir, Ivanovo, Kostroma, Yaroslavl, Kalinin, Smolensk, Kaluga, Bryansk, Orel, Tula, and Ryazan.

Winters are severe in the northern part of this region. Snow lies across it from the middle of November to the beginning of April. The average January temperature in Moscow is 14° F., but it may sink to—40° F. In the southern part of the area (Tula, Orel, Ryazan) the climate is milder.

The country here is a gently rolling plain and is called Central Russian Uplands. In the north, especially beyond the Volga River, there are still large forests of spruce and pine. In the center and the south, only patches of woods are left, consisting of birch, aspen, oak, and pine. Because of this the brown bear, former lord of the woods, has retreated to the north. The wolf, the lynx, the fox, the badger are still there and many species of birds.

The land abounds in rivers and in lakes and swamps, especially in the northern part. The Volga, most important (though not the longest) Russian river, rises in a swamp in the Valdai Hills of the Kalinin Province. It crosses the region in a zigzagging line from west to east. The province is also crossed by a large tributary of the Volga, the Oka, and by smaller rivers of the Volga-Oka system, such as the Klyazama and the Moskva. Here, too, in the Smolensk and the Tula Provinces respectively, are the origins of two other great Russian rivers, the Dnieper and the Don. Due to the region's relative flatness, the drainage is poor. In the spring these rivers flood wide areas, shining like giant mirrors in the sun. For this reason both peasant villages and cities are usually situated on the rivers' elevated, hilly banks.

The Central Industrial Region is densely peopled, with 27 million inhabitants, or about 150 per square mile. Though the area forms but 2.2 percent of the Soviet Union's total territory, over 12 percent of the entire population live here. There are also more cities (228 in all) than in any other part of the Soviet Union of similar size. In some places they form practically uninterrupted chains.

Virtually all of the population here are of Great Russian stock. An average Russian is not necessarily very tall; he is stocky and very muscular, usually blond, and often has broad cheekbones. Until recently, one of the peasant's favorite sports was to hunt the brown bear in the woods, single-handed and armed with just a pikelike stick sharpened at one end (*rogátina.*) Born woodsmen, Great Russian peasants, both in this area and elsewhere, usually live in log cabins.

About 67 percent of the region's population are city-dwellers engaged in industry, transport services, or Government service. For the region's cities are important industrial centers. Virtually all manufacturing industries are represented here: watchmaking, textiles, synthetic rubber, oil refining, metalworking, building of machines and machine tools, construction of automobiles and locomotives. Moscow alone accounts for 8 percent of the Soviet Union's total industrial production, and the cotton mills of the Ivanovo Province produce a larger amount of cotton tissues than all of Great Britain. Textiles are the region's oldest industry.

The remaining 33 percent of the region's population are farmers. On this land the major crops are hemp, flax, and potatoes. Hemp and flax are planted chiefly in the northern provinces, as these crops are needed for the region's great textile mills. Potatoes are an important item of the Russians' diet. Vodka, the national Russian alcoholic beverage, is distilled from potatoes. And it is out of potato alcohol, too, that synthetic rubber is made for the great Yaroslavl automobile tire plant.

Other farm produce comes from vegetable gardens, dairy farms, and animal husbandry, for consumption in nearby cities. One sees also rye and barley fields where tractors are at work. Wheat and beetroot are grown chiefly in the warmer southern provinces of the region.

Despite its great economic importance, the Central Industrial Region is poor in its own natural resources. Its chief resource is the brown coal of the Moscow Coal Basin, occupying a wide area north, south, and southeast of Moscow itself. But this coal, though good for heating and for generating electricity, does not make coke and cannot be used in metallurgy. Also there are iron ore deposits near Tula, which have been exploited since the seventeenth century. Some of the clays found in the region are good for bricks and for ceramics. Aside from these there are only peat and scattered deposits of phosphate rock. The latter is used for agricultural fertilizers.

This region poor in natural resources has acquired such a great economic importance chiefly because its main city is Moscow. This region in general, and Moscow in particular, has been for centuries Russia's very heart and nerve-center. Out of them the entire Russian State has been built.

Originally, Moscow was only a tiny fortress and trading post. But its wooden walls had been built at the confluence of the Moskva and the Yáuza rivers, close to the Volga and the Oka. It thus lay at the crossing of important river trade routes.

In 1237–40, when the Tartar-Mongol hordes swept down from Asia, Moscow, like most other Russian cities, was sacked and burned. But from the beginning of the fourteenth century, Moscow took the lead over other Russian lands. Its princes proved to be shrewd and far-sighted. They paid tribute to the Tartar-Mongol khan and patiently built up their strength, while the Golden Horde was being weakened by internal dissent. They became Russia's grand dukes. Gradually they welded separate Russian principalities into one centralized state. Finally, in 1380, Grand Duke Dimitry inflicted a smashing defeat on the entire Tartar-Mongol army. Dimitry became a national hero. Moscow's role as Russia's capital was henceforth unchallenged. That was the beginning of the defeat of the Tartar Yoke.

In 1485–1495 the wooden walls of the Moscow Kremlin—or inner fortress with its palaces and cathedrals—were replaced by massive walls, which stand to this day. In the following centuries, three more belts of fortification grew up around the Kremlin. For as Moscow expanded, its commercial, industrial, and residential sections, too, required protection from the enemy. In modern times, these outlying fortifications have been razed and have given place to wide, circular boulevards. Thus, Moscow's entire present layout—that of streets radiating in all directions from the center (the Kremlin)—has been determined by the city's history.

In the sixteenth century Moscow was the largest Russian city, with well over 200,000 inhabitants. As the seat of the country's government and of the court of the grand dukes (called tsars since 1547) it attracted a multitude not only of noble families, courtiers and soldiers, but also of merchants, tradesmen, and craftsmen. Whole quarters or streets of the city were—and still are—named after them: the Weavers (*Khamovniki*), the Armorers (*Bronniki*), the Boilermakers (*Kotelniki*). And Moscow's Trade Rows—its great bazaar—was renowned, in the sixteenth and seventeenth centuries, in many countries of the world. East and West met there. There one could buy anything. Thus, Moscow's political role made it also Russia's natural and most important economic center.

Although, in 1714, Tsar Peter the Great transferred Russia's capital to St. Petersburg, Moscow retained its immense economic importance. It was primarily in Moscow that he encouraged the creation of "modern" European-type factories—such as those for textiles, cloth, and leather. It was here, in the center of the Empire, that demand for manufactured goods was especially great.

In 1861 Russian peasants were liberated from their position as serfs and given land of their own. This gave a powerful spurt to Russia's further development. Many of the former serfs flocked to cities, especially to Moscow, in search of industrial work. New factories, mills, and railroads began to spring up. Moscow rapidly began to acquire (at least in the center) the looks of a modern city. Its population grew from 350,000 in 1863 to 1,800,000 in 1917.

In the long centuries of its existence, Moscow often was attacked. During the Interregnum and the Time of Troubles of 1610–1613, it was occupied—and much of it was burned—by the Poles. In 1812, Napoleon I, Emperor of the French and one of the greatest strategists of all times, fought his way into Moscow. But now the Russians *themselves* burned their great city, rather than let the invader have it. About three-fourths of Moscow's buildings were consumed by flames. Instead of "dictating peace in Moscow" to Russia's Emperor Alexander I, as Napoleon had proposed to do, he had to withdraw his starving and freezing army from the city's charred ruins. The retreat of the Grande Armée over Russia's snow-covered wastes, with the Russians relentlessly bleeding it white by numberless raids, was the beginning of the French Army's end—and of Napoleon's undoing.

In 1941, Hitler's huge Nazi army, spearheaded by thirteen tank divisions, drove, after a series of severe and bloody battles, to within fifteen to twenty-four miles of Moscow. Here the Nazis were stopped dead by the Soviet Army and turned back. It was their *first* heavy defeat in World War II.

Today Moscow, one of the world's great cities, houses 6,500,000 inhabitants (compared to New York's 7,960,000). It is a city of contrasts. Besides some of the tall glass-and-chromium buildings and blocks of five- to twelve-story modern—and monotonous—apartment houses built of concrete blocks, it still has quite a few wooden or stucco one- or two-story houses, reminding one of its wooden past. The Kremlin's enclave with its complex of buildings—fifteenth- to seventeenth-century palaces, cathedrals, churches, whose golden cupolas soar into the sky like captive balloons—is a unique sight. At night, five red stars, emblems of the Soviet Union, gleam on its towers. Remarkable, too, are other historical buildings scattered in the city, from the flamboyant St. Basil Cathedral to palatial mansions which belonged to wealthy noblemen before the Revolution and now are museums or other institutions. The Moskva River, framed in granite quays and snaking through the city, adds to Moscow's looks.

The Soviet Union's ruling Communist Party emphatically disapproves of all religions. Hence, while old church buildings of artistic or historical value are being preserved as such, most of them are no longer used as *active churches*. No divine services are held in them. They are merely museums—and, in some cases, storage buildings or cinemas.

As Moscow is the capital, in the Kremlin's palaces gather the Soviet Union's Supreme Soviet (equivalent to our Congress) and the Council of Ministers (corresponding to our President's Cabinet). Besides these, numerous other government institutions are located in the city.

Moscow is also Russia's great intellectual center. It is, as it were, symbolized by the impressive 32-story new main building of the Moscow University. But all told nearly eighty high educational institutions, attended by 200,000 students—both full time and through correspondence—are located in the city. Here, too, are various departments of the Academy of Sciences, libraries, over one hundred museums and the best Russian theaters, including the *Bolshoi* Theatre.

Especially important is Moscow's role as a center of the Soviet Union's transportation system. Numerous air routes, eleven railroads, and fourteen automobile roads converge on it from all parts of the Soviet Union—the Ukraine, Siberia, the sunny Caucasus, and the Arctic belt. A very large part of goods circulating in the Soviet Union—be it grain, canned fish products, oil, electrical appliances, or various sophisticated machinery—do so by way of Moscow.

Moscow is served by yet another great transportation artery—the Moscow Canal. Moskva River was too shallow for modern riverboats.

Hence, to provide Russia's capital with a really navigable waterway, the Soviet Government completed, in 1937, the 76-mile-long Moscow Canal. It joins Moskva River in Moscow with the upper Volga due north, near Ivankovo. It is equipped with great dams, eight locks, three large hydroelectric power plants, and artificial reservoirs or "inland seas," in which water is collected. With their aid, water level in the Moskva has been raised so that now 3500-ton ships navigate in it.

Freighters, tankers, passenger boats with vacationers, tourists and school children's excursion boats—daily descend Moskva River, by way of the Oka, to the lower Volga, or ascend the Canal's locks to the upper Volga. The Volga, which flows into the Caspian Sea, is linked by navigable canals to other rivers also, draining into the White, the Baltic, the Azov, and the Black seas. Hence, Moscow has been nicknamed a "port of the five seas."

Transportation by water is far less costly than by rail so the Canal's role is an important one. Moscow receives by river chiefly bulky goods—grain, salt, oil, cotton, vegetables, building materials. From Moscow these boats carry industrial equipment, machines, cars, consumer goods, and products of food industries to outlying areas.

Those who sail on the Volga downstream from Ivankovo soon find themselves in a huge, sealike body of water. It is the sea or reservoir of Rybinsk. This was formed in 1941 by the construction of dams on the Volga and its tributary, the Sheksna. With a surface area of about 1,300 square miles, it was at the time the largest man-made reservoir in the world. Along the lower Volga, Soviet engineers later constructed still larger ones. Before the depression which now holds the Sea of Rybinsk began filling with water, the population of a number of villages that lay in it had been relocated, and these villages were flooded.

The reservoir has greatly improved the old waterway linking the Volga to the Baltic Sea. Electricity generated by the mighty hydroelectric power plant of Rybinsk is used to operate the locks, and is also supplied at low rates to the Yaroslavl, Kalinin, and Moscow provinces.

Let us now glance at just a few of the many other cities of the area. The second largest to Moscow is Yaroslavl, "the Soviet Akron," with a population of 500,000. Founded in 1024, it still preserves quite a few relics of the past. Two of the towers of its sixteenth-century kremlin stand intact. So do some homes and remarkable churches and

Chapter II
THE CENTRAL INDUSTRIAL REGION

0   25   50   75   100
MILES

"Sea of Rybinsk" Reservoir

SHEEPSKIN COATS

SAW MILLS

RYBINSK

KOSTROMA

YAROSLAVL

UGLICH

COTTON MILLS

IVANOVO

VALDAI HILLS

Lake Seliger

RAILROAD EQUIPMENT

KALININ

Volga River

FLAX

Moscow Canal

DUBNA
United Institute of Nuclear Research

VLADIMIR

BARLEY

OATS

St. BASIL

MOSCOW

Klyazma River

OREKHOVO

MOSCOW UNIVERSITY

Moskva River

COAL

HEMP

Dnieper River

HEAVY INDUSTRY

BOG IRON ORE

SERPUKHOV

Oka River

RYAZAN

RAIL CENTER

SMOLENSK

ORE SMELTERY
KALUGA

TEXTILES

VEGETABLES AND

YASNAYA POLYANA

TULA

FRUIT

FLAX

SUGAR BEETS

SAMOVARS

Don River

BRYANSK

Oka River

OREL

MANUFACTURING

WHEAT

monasteries of that period. In Yaroslavl the first Russian professional theater was founded in the middle of the eighteenth century. The first flax textile mill in Russia was set up here in 1722, a mill that has been transformed by the Soviet Government into a large textile combine. The city has a plant for making synthetic rubber, heavy truck motors, diesel engines, electrical equipment, and various other works. It is one of the most industrialized cities in the Soviet Union.

Kalinin (310,000) was formerly known as Tver. In the fourteenth and early fifteenth centuries, it was the capital of an important principality, which competed with that of Moscow for the role of the leader of Russian lands. Now it produces railroad rolling stock, bulldozers, and equipment for textile mills. Overlooking, as it does, the Volga from its elevated right bank, the city is quite picturesque.

The little city of Dubna houses the internationally known United Institute of Nuclear Research for peaceful purposes. Scientists of each of the twelve nations represented in it have research laboratories of their own. Dubna is but one of the "academic cities," of which quite a few have lately appeared in different regions of the Soviet Union. Each academic city is devoted to some specific branch of science— nuclear physics, genetics, geology, radio-wave propagation. Specialists live there and carry on advanced research in such subjects, in well-equipped research institutes.

One of the main cities in the Central Industrial Region's southwest is Smolensk (183,000). Over 1,100 years old, it is probably the oldest Russian city. It lies close to the watershed between the Baltic and the Black seas drainage basins. On their way to Constantinople, the Varengians (Scandinavians) sailed the rivers of the Baltic basin up to that watershed, hauled their boats overland and, near Smolensk, hit the Dnieper, whose waters carried them to the Black Sea.

Smolensk lies on the route of invasions from the West toward Moscow. It changed hands between Moscovy and Poland-Lithuania time after time. In 1812, during Napoleon's march on Moscow, Smolensk, after a stubborn three-day battle, was reduced to charred ruins. And in 1941, during World War II, an exceptionally bloody battle between the Nazi and the Soviet armies went on there for weeks. As a result, official Soviet sources say Smolensk was "90 percent annihilated." After the war, it was virtually built anew.

Sitting in a predominantly flax-growing country, Smolensk engages primarily in textile industry: it has a large flax combinat (that is, coordinated set of mills or factories). It also produces road-building equipment, has shoe factories, and is an important rail center, where five railways cross.

The largest city in the south of the region is Tula (370,000 inhabitants). In the sixteenth and seventeenth centuries Tula was one of the key points in the defense line of moats, ramparts, and felled trees which protected Moscow from Tartar raids. Tula is Russia's oldest metallurgical center. In the seventeenth century, the first "modern" blast furnaces and foundries in Russia were set up in and around the city by two Dutch businessmen who had settled in Muscovy. A century later, Peter the Great built the Tula armaments plant, which long remained the largest in the country. Now Tula produces modern agricultural machinery, road-building equipment, sewing machines. It also continues to produce sundry metalware and, in particular, harmonicas and the famed Russian *samovars*. (A *samovar* is a metal vessel, with a heating tube in the center, used by the Russians for heating water for tea, and the teapot itself is placed at the top of the tube.)

A few miles south of Tula lies Yasnaya Polyana, country estate of Count Leo Tolstoy, great nineteenth-century Russian fiction writer and moral philosopher. His moral prestige was such that, in his lifetime, he was referred to as "the world's conscience." The Soviet Government has transformed Tolstoy's modest manor house into a national museum and carefully preserves it.

3

★

THE CENTRAL
BLACK EARTH REGION

Immediately south of the Central Industrial Region is an area which resembles it, the Central Black Earth Region. This is a land with the same gently rolling terrain, the same open countryside with ravines and rivers, and with sparse woods, passing in the south into continuous plowlands (except along the Don River), and the same villages of log cabins. The region is made up of five provinces: Kursk, Belgorod, Lipetsk, Voronezh, and Tambov.

However, the climate here is considerably milder, and the soil is far more fertile. Wheat, corn, sugar beet, sunflower, and *makhorka* (popular low-grade tobacco), grow well here. Besides these, the crops cultivated around Moscow or Kalinin—potatoes, hemp, and vegetables—are grown here, too. There is also much dairy farming, cattle breeding, and raising of pigs, sheep, and poultry. It is here that one of the best Russian horses, the Orlov trotter, is bred. The woods and parks of the region, especially in the Kursk Province, are filled with nightingales. From May to August the nightingales' concerts are incomparably beautiful here.

The bulk of the population here, just as in the preceding region, is Great Russian. Only in the southwest of the Kursk Province are there also Ukrainian areas.

The region's mineral resources are limited. Except for phosphates and various building materials, including cement clay, it has but one very important asset, the Kursk Magnetic Anomaly, or KMA.

As early as 1783 a Russian scientist pointed out that in the Kursk region the magnetic needle dipped, as though drawn to earth by a powerful magnet. This indicated the presence of large deposits of iron ore. But it was not until 1919–1926 that a thorough magnetic survey of the KMA was carried out. It revealed apparently the largest accumulation of iron ore, chiefly magnetite quartzite, in the world, 9,000 billion tons. It lies in streaks, running for some 280 miles, across the provinces of Bryansk, Kursk, Belgorod, and Voronezh.

Much of that ore has a relatively low iron content. But at least 50 billion tons—in particular in the areas of Belgorod, Old Oskol, and New Oskol—are easily accessible high-grade ore with an iron content of 54–69 percent. The Soviet Government has organized its extraction on a large scale.

Much of the region's surplus agricultural products are consumed by the obvious next-door market, the Central Industrial Region. Out of the Black Earth Region's population of 8 million, 67 percent are country dwellers (chiefly collective farmers) and only 33 percent are city people. There are important industrial and cultural centers here, too. But they are far less numerous than in the Moscow, Yaroslavl, or Vladimir provinces.

The northern part of the Black Earth Region was settled early by the Russians. Kursk was in existence already in the eleventh century. But then many Russian settlements here were wiped out by the Crimean Tartars.

In the early fifteenth century, the Tartar Golden Horde, formerly united, split into several Mohammedan khanates, or kingdoms, and hordes. One was the Khanate of the Crimea, on the peninsula of the same name which juts out into the Black Sea. In the fifteenth to seventeenth centuries this was a real bandits' nest which throve and prospered on the systematic plunder of Muscovy. Mounted Tartar hordes yearly crossed the wide no-man's-land or "wild field," separating the Crimea from Muscovy. They often managed to bypass the main Russian forces and penetrated deep into the country. There they fanned out, sacked, murdered, and set the torch to crops, villages, cities, drove away cattle and abducted thousands of prisoners, whom they sold into slavery.

A perfect springboard for attacks on Muscovy, the Crimea itself was all but impregnable to Muscovite armies. The Tartars had strongly fortified the narrow isthmus attaching their peninsula to the mainland. In case of Russian attacks, they withdrew behind it. And the Russians could not carry on a long siege far from their homeland, where they lacked water and fodder for horses. Furthermore, Crimean khans were vassals of the Turkish sultans, who, dominating the Black Sea, often helped them with their armies. Moscow rulers were compelled to transform their southern borderland, the present-day Black Earth Region, into a defensive zone. They built several defensive lines in the area. Noblemen, peasants, and Cossacks were settled in the area to create an on-the-spot defense force to delay, if not to stop, the Tartars.

These lines of stubborn Russians gradually advanced against the Tartars. By the middle of the seventeenth century the foremost Russian fortified line had descended some 120 miles south, to Belgorod-

Voronezh-Tambov. It was a slow, year-in, year-out battle, during which many Muscovite squires and Cossacks literally "lived in the saddle." It claimed many human lives, and many manor houses and villages were reduced to ashes. But in that war the tsars stubbornly, relentlessly pushed Muscovy's borders and Russian settlements farther south, conquering new portions of the "wild field."

By the late eighteenth century the southern steppe was well settled by Russians. Tartar raids—sometimes serious ones—still did occur. But in 1783 Empress Catherine the Great's commanders overcame the Tartars' resistance. The Crimea was annexed to the Russian Empire.

Russian cities of the region had little economic value. Nor were they close to important river trade routes. The main river, the Don, was a blind alley, for it drained into the Azov Sea by the great Turkish fortress of Azov. Most cities of the region started out as mere strong points in the wild field. Such was the case of Voronezh (built in 1586), of Belgorod (1583), of Tambov (1636). It was only with time that they began to play an economic and cultural role as well as a political one.

Today Voronezh, the region's largest city, has a population of 560,000. It has outstanding institutions of higher education, good theaters, large industrial plants. It also holds an important place in food industry, especially in sugar refining. An atomic power plant is under construction in the city. Voronezh is bisected by the Voronezh River, an affluent of the Don, and its valley, about one and a half miles wide. Within the city an island rises out of the river.

Peter the great gave the first impetus to Voronezh's economic development by using it as Russia's main base in its wars of 1695–1696 with Turkey. He built a foundry, a rope-yard, and a cloth mill. A large, beautifully proportioned military storehouse, as well as the remarkable Cathedral of Assumption and some other relics of Peter's time, stood in Voronezh until recently, when the city was virtually wiped off the face of the earth.

During World War II, from July, 1942, to January, 1943, the front-line bisected Voronezh. The half of the city on the right, elevated bank of the river was held by the Nazis; its opposite side remained in the hands of the Soviet Army. Both sides were the sites of stubborn battles and continual artillery barrages. When the Germans were rolled back, 97 percent of the city's buildings were in ruins. Voronezh as it stands today, including its modern industrial plants, universities, and apartment houses, has been built anew.

Since the time of Peter the Great Lipetsk (230,000) has been an important metallurgical center. Its Novolipetsky Combinat, recently built by the Soviets and using the KMA ore for the full-cycle production of pig-iron-steel-rolled steel, is one of the largest metallurgical plants in the European part of the RSFSR. Tractor construction, chemical, building materials, and other industries are represented here. Mineral springs near Lipetsk—whose value was first grasped by Peter —make the city a well-known Soviet watering place.

In the region's rural areas one sees a great many peasant villages. They are much alike in most Great Russian parts of the RSFSR.

An average Russian village has a dozen to a hundred—or even a thousand—*izby*, or log cabins, aligned on one or both sides of a wide dirt road. (Concrete or asphalt roads are comparatively rare in the Soviet Union.) Its size may depend upon various factors. In the past, *safety* meant a great deal in village planning for a large village could defend itself from raiders better than a tiny hamlet. If there was no city in the vicinity, a large village tended to become a much-needed trading center. Hence, in the south, including the Black Earth Region, peasants grouped into larger settlements. Closer to Moscow, villages were smaller. The type of villages developed four hundred to five hundred years ago linger on to this day.

On the fringe of a larger village usually stands a church with a cemetery beside it. Now it is likely to have been closed, or even torn down, under the pressure of the Communist Party. Russian peasants always were—and many still are despite the Communists—very religious.

Peasant *izby* are usually unpainted one-story structures. An average *izba* has a tall two-slope roof of boards (iron roofs are rare) and three tiny windows in the wall facing the road. They are separated by muddy spaces where pigs, chickens, and ducks live. Behind the houses lie kitchen gardens.

Russian Slavs of the wooded belt have lived in such *izby* for hundreds of years. They were already in existence in the eighth and ninth centuries. Lately, with the construction by the Soviet Government of a number of large hydroelectric power plants, electricity has penetrated into the countryside. Radio and television sets have been ap-

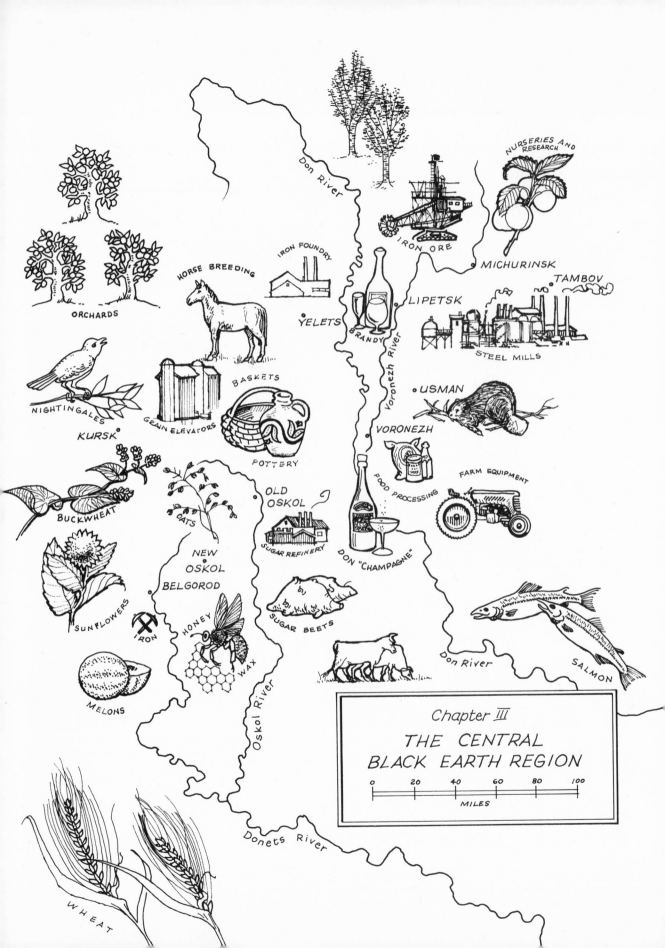

ORCHARDS

NURSERIES AND RESEARCH

MICHURINSK

HORSE BREEDING

IRON FOUNDRY

Don River

IRON ORE

TAMBOV

LIPETSK

YELETS

BRANDY

Voronezh River

STEEL MILLS

NIGHTINGALES

BASKETS

USMAN

KURSK

GRAIN ELEVATORS

POTTERY

VORONEZH

FARM EQUIPMENT

BUCKWHEAT

OATS

OLD OSKOL

FOOD PROCESSING

SUNFLOWERS

NEW OSKOL

SUGAR REFINERY

BELGOROD

DON "CHAMPAGNE"

IRON

HONEY

SUGAR BEETS

MELONS

WAX

Oskol River

Don River

SALMON

Chapter III

THE CENTRAL
BLACK EARTH REGION

0   20   40   60   80   100

MILES

Donets River

WHEAT

pearing in the *izby*. Today, however, houses, resembling modern suburban cottages, are gradually replacing the old *izby*.

A few neighboring villages usually belong to the same *kolkhoz*, or collective farm. Before the Revolution, each peasant family worked on its own plot. But in 1928–32 the Soviet Government urged—often even forced—peasants to pool their land, most of their livestock, and their other means of production. The Communist Party holds that more advanced agricultural machinery and methods can be used on large collective farms rather than on small individual holdings.

In many regions peasants stubbornly opposed collectivization. They did not want to become, as they put it, government employees on large farms, which would be closely controlled by Soviet authorities. In some areas they even rose in revolts, which were suppressed by armed force. As a concession, peasants were allowed to retain small individual allotments for whatever vegetables, poultry, etc., they needed for themselves or might wish to sell. It is these allotments, or parts of them, that one usually sees behind their cabins. Also, the peasants' position on collective farms has greatly improved recently.

Often the stately nearby manor house of the former landowner, dispossessed after the Revolution of 1917, serves as the collective farms' administrative center, meeting hall for the farmers, or school for their children.

4

★

THE VOLGA REGION

The irregularly oblong territory lying along the middle and the lower course of the great Volga River is called *Povolzhye* by the Russians, but we know it as the Volga Region, or Volgaland.

It is equal, roughly, to the area of Texas and Wyoming combined. It stretches from the Central Industrial Region and the headwaters of Kama River (the Volga's main tributary) in the north to the Caspian Sea in the south.

This vast region combines different climates typified by a sharp contrast, typical of continental climates, between very cold winters and hot summers. In Kazan, for instance, the average temperatures for January and July are, respectively, 7.6° F. and 67.8° F. The south of the region suffers from lack of rainfall.

The region also crosses different geographical zones. There is the stern, northern landscape of great coniferous forests of pine and fir standing guard over the high, rocky right bank of the Kama; endless, undulating wheat fields around Saratov; the steppes of silverlike feather-grass near Kamyshin; and arid, sun-scorched Kalmyk deserts between Volgograd and the Caspian shore, dotted with patches of salt marshes.

The Volga Region is an important and interesting part of Russia. It has a great natural wealth, a large agricultural production, and powerful and varied industries. It has a population of 26 millions, of whom one-quarter are of ethnically non-Russian stock. These non-Russian peoples form an ethnical "crazy quilt" of six small Autonomous Soviet Socialist Republics, or ASSR's.

From north to southeast they are: the Mari, the Chuvash, the Mordovian, the Tartar, the Bashkir and the Kalmyk ASSR's. Surrounding the republics are the predominantly Russian provinces of Kirov, Gorky, Ulyanovsk, Penza, Kuibyshev, Saratov, Volgograd, and Astrakhan.

One of the Volga Region's peculiarities is that modern Europe blends there with medieval Asia. In Ufa or Volgograd, for instance, there are up-to-date universities, theaters, and industrial plants. But only a few miles away, nomadic Mohammedan or Buddhist cattle-breeders still live in their felt tents, just as their ancestors lived in the tenth or twelfth centuries.

The Volga is a natural economic axis holding the region's various sections together. The river, 2,300 miles long, is the longest in Europe. It is the most powerful transportation artery in the Soviet Union, and the region's industries and agriculture naturally gravitate to it. Most of the region's numerous large cities—Gorky, Kazan, Kuibyshev, and Saratov—nestle on the river's banks, especially at points of its intersection with railways.

Most Russian rivers which flow south have a high right bank and a low, flat left bank. Thus most Volga cities and villages sit on its right bank. The whole country back of the elevated bank is cut by ravines. This is the Volga Uplands, a geological extension of the Central Russian Uplands.

The region's most important natural resource is oil. The great Volga-Urals oil deposits are scattered over a 600-mile area along the Kama River, its tributary, the Belaya, and the Volga itself, from Perm (in the Ural Mountains) to Volgograd. Some of the best fields lie in the Kuibyshev-Syzran and Saratov areas and in the Tartar and Bashkir ASSR's. Farther north, the deposits pass into the Urals proper.

The presence of oil has been recorded here since the eighteenth century. Before the Revolution asphalt was already produced along the Volga. It was only in 1929 that oil was struck near Chussovskiye Gorodki, in the Urals. Three years later, it was found at Ishimbayev (Bashkir ASSR). In 1935 it gushed north of Syzran, near Kuibyshev. It was only then that actual exploitation began. The Soviet Government opened the oil fields with great energy, and the yield of the Volga-Urals fields grew fast. They account for 65 percent of Russia's total yearly output of 224 million tons.

Refineries for Volgaland oil are located in Gorky, Kuibyshev, Syzran, Saratov, Volgograd, and Ufa. At least two of them—in Ufa and Saratov—were built with American engineering help. Much of the region's petroleum and natural gas goes by pipelines to European and Asiatic Russia. One of them, the Friendship Pipeline, conveys petroleum from Kuibyshev to Soviet allies—Poland, East Germany, Hungary, Czechoslovakia. Some of it is also shipped to various destinations in Volga tankers.

The northern Kirov Province and Mari ASSR, both lying in the forest zone, produce a great deal of lumber and pulp. In the Bashkir ASSR, copper, zinc, silver, gold, iron ore, and brown coal are mined. Along the lower-middle Volga, there are clays from which immense quantities of cement are produced in Volsk.

In the region's powerful and rapidly developing manufacturing industries, the leading place belongs to various types of machine-building from locomotives to calculators. Chemical industry and the production of fertilizers, synthetic rubber, and artificial fibers are also important.

The Volgaland is of great importance to the Soviet Union's agriculture. The 250-mile-wide transition wooded steppe zone—from Kazan to Volsk—is a great producer of rye, millet, potatoes, hemp, and some fruit, such as apples and cherries.

However, it is the next 250 miles of the steppe zone to the south with its extra fertile "black soil"—especially in the Saratov Province—that form the region's real granary. This is wheat country above all. The undulating fields stretch as far as the eye can see and yield immense crops.

Occasionally this agricultural belt experiences severe droughts. The *sukhovey*, the arid wind rising in the deserts on the Asiatic side of the Caspian Sea, begins to blow. A scorching mist, or thin dust, fills the air. The sun shines through it like a red-hot ball. If the *sukhovey* has blown for two to three days on end, it leaves the flourishing, prosperous countryside literally roasted. The territory on the left of the river suffers especially. For the high right bank does offer some protection from the *sukhovey*.

While such droughts are not a yearly occurrence, various anti-drought measures are being taken. Water from thawing snow is collected in ponds, and protective forest belts have been planted.

Finally, other items of the Volga Region's wealth are fish and caviar. The fisheries in the river's estuary around Astrakhan rate among the richest in the world.

The growing importance of the Volga Region has made great demands on the river as a means of transportation. During the seven- or eight-month-long ice-free season, millions of tons of goods plus hundreds of thousands of passengers go up and down the river.

Until recently not all of the Volga was equally good for navigation. Over a mile wide between Gorky and Kazan and still wider farther down, it was, for long stretches, also quite deep. But the river's gradient is very small, and its course sluggish. Hence, it had shoals and sandbanks which obstructed the passage of larger craft.

Since the 1930's, the Soviet Government has carried out an ambitious project of reconstruction of the Volga and some of its tributaries. The object has been greatly to increase that system's traffic capacity, making it navigable for large river craft.

The Volga has now been cut by mammoth dams, equipped with locks and with powerful hydroelectric power plants. Electricity operates the locks, whose function is to raise or lower ships from one water level to another.

Each of these dams greatly raises the level of the Volga before it. It thus backs up an immense inland sea, or reservoir, two to four hundred miles long and quite a few miles wide. Such are the "seas" of Volgograd, of Kuibyshev, of Gorky. The Volga has been transformed into a staircase of connected reservoirs with lakelike conditions of navigation, for they are much deeper than was the original river. Ships up to 3,500 tons ply them. On stormy days, waves in the reservoirs rise to a height of eight feet and more.

Now the Volga has the traffic capacity of ten to twelve first-class railways. In the Central Industrial Region the upper Volga, similarly reconstructed, is linked to Moscow by the Moscow Canal and to rivers draining into the Baltic and the White seas. In the south, near Volgograd, the Volga has been connected by a large canal to the Don River, which links it to the Azov and the Black seas. Thus, the Volga is a mighty throughway crossing the entire European part of the Soviet Union from north to south. This lends a great added economic importance to the Volga Region.

The Volga Region became part of Russia only in the sixteenth century, but its history goes back to the Neolithic (or late Stone) Age. Remnants of camps of the neolithic man and his polished stone tools have been found all along the Volga. In the fifth century B.C., Herodotus, the Greek historian, described the Volga, which he called *Rha*.

Since the dawn of our era, the river has fulfilled the same function as it does now. It served as a waterway connecting the Asiatic peoples of the Caspian Sea area, the Volga Region's native Finnish tribes, the Russian Slavs, and the Scandinavians.

Peoples emerging from Asia through the flat steppes south of the Urals collided and succeeded one another in the Volga Region. In the 1430's, two Tartar Khanates, Kazan and Astrakhan, were established on the middle and the lesser Volga. They were two of the splinters into which the once powerful Golden Horde had disintegrated. The situation along Moscow's eastern border became similar to the bitter struggle between Tartars and Russians along its southern wild field.

In 1552, Tsar Ivan the Terrible took Kazan after a great and victorious battle. Four years later, Muscovite troops floated down the Volga in boats and took Astrakhan, capital of the second Tartar Khanate on the great river.

Thus the Russians won a decisive victory over the Tartars in the Volga Region two centuries earlier than in the Crimea. But warlike and unsubdued nomadic peoples remained east of the Volga and along its middle-lower course.

The tsars built defensive lines and fortresses here much as they did in the south. Some of the defensive lines were an extension of the southern ones. The tsars donated large landed estates in the newly conquered country to their noblemen who settled their serfs on them. The Tartar, Mordovian, and Bashkir nobles were also allowed to keep their status and their lands, provided they would serve the tsars. Eventually many embraced Christianity and became fully "Russified."

Finally, settlers from all over Russia, and sometimes even from foreign European countries, were encouraged to come to the region.

But the region remained unsettled. Nogai Tartars and Kazakhs often raided the new Russian estates. The Cossacks, who had begun to settle on the Yaik (now the Ural) River since the sixteenth century, were supported, to some extent, by Moscow, for they, too, helped to Russify the land. But they attacked both the Nogais and Kazakhs, and caravans of Russian merchants sailing down the Volga. Moreover, there was much discontent among the peasants, and the malcontents from elsewhere in Russia fled to the Volga.

Two mammoth peasant uprisings shook the region in 1670–71 and in 1773–75, headed by two audacious Cossack adventurers.

It was only in the nineteenth century that the Volga Region became an organic part of Russia. It long remained—perhaps still remains— to many Russians a symbol of freedom and of the spirit of opportunity and adventure.

At the Volga Region's western fringe lies its largest city (and fifth largest in the Soviet Union)—Gorky, with a population of 1,100,000. It is an oil-refining center and a great center of heavy industry, turning out automobiles, river ships, aircraft, milling machines, chemical plant equipment. Its large automobile plant, which makes Zim cars, was built in 1932 by American engineers sent over by Henry Ford. The great Sormov Plant, producing river ships and locomotives, was built in 1849.

With its ten institutions of higher learning—among them a university and various specialized research institutes—Gorky is also an important intellectual center. Once called Nizhny Novgorod, the city was renamed to honor Maxim Gorky, a famous Russian writer, who was born there in 1868. Gorky lies at the junction of the Volga and the Oka and is one of the main river ports of the region. It is one of the loveliest Russian cities, descending in terraces from the Volga's elevated right bank to the river itself. After the conquest of Kazan by Ivan the Terrible in 1552, Nizhny became one of the Volga Region's most important centers. This was mainly because of its famed Fair, a peculiar and colorful feature of Old Russia's life. Merchants from all over Russia, from China, Persia, other Asiatic and some European countries flocked to the Nizhny Fair. Along with serious business there was gargantuan merrymaking. The Fair was part of Imperial Russia's life. With the suppression of private capital by the Soviets, it came to an end.

Eighty miles down the Volga from Gorky begins the ethnical crazy quilt of the Volga Region's autonomous republics. Five of them are grouped together.

The Mari ASSR lies mostly on the river's left bank. There are 510,000 Maris in the Soviet Union, of whom 270,000 live—together with Russians, Tartars, and others—in their own small republic. It is a poor country, lying in the forest zone which extends to the river's edge. Its main assets are the forests of pine, spruce, and silver fir, that occupy half of its territory. Lumbering, woodworking, and pulp-and-paper industries are the major industries. At Yoshkar-Ola, the republic's capital (population 126,000), there is also agricultural machinery construction, furniture-making, and vitamin production. In deforested sections, rye, potatoes, and flax are sown. Kozmodemyansk, on the Volga's right bank, is an important river port for timber.

The Maris are direct descendants of the Volga Region's original Finnish tribes. They were subjugated by the Tartars and absorbed into Muscovy, but they still retain their national identity.

Considerably to the south with no direct access to the Volga, lies the tiny Mordovian ASSR. Also a Finnish people, the Mordovians are nationally, linguistically, and historically the Maris' close kin. There are 1,285,000 Mordovians in the Soviet Union. Only 310,000 live in Mordovia, whose total population is 1,000,000. The rest are scattered, in ethnical groups, over other parts of the Volga Region and elsewhere. Mordovia thrives chiefly on agriculture (including spring wheat and sugar beet growing), as well as on flour milling, distilling, and woodworking. After World War II modern electrical, machine-building and other plants have grown up in its capital, Saransk (124,000).

Some Mari and Mordovian peasant women still wear their ancient national dress, a long, straight shirt with much embroidery on the shoulder, sleeves, and front, worn over wide pants. Married women always cover their hair. Many Mordovians and Maris did not become Christians until the nineteenth century.

Individual members of these peoples learned Russian long ago and even played a role in Russia's intellectual life. But until recently they had no written language of their own. This was worked out only after the Revolution of 1917, with the help of Russian scholars. Now in both republics there is a network of native primary and secondary schools. In Saransk, there are also three Mordovian institutions of

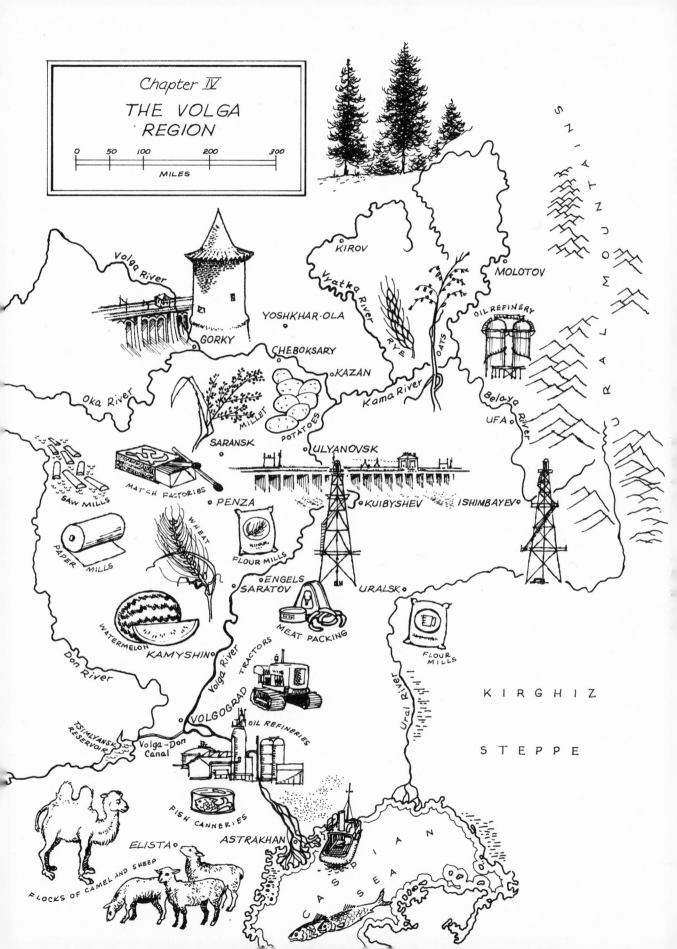

Chapter IV

THE VOLGA REGION

0   50   100   200   300

MILES

KIROV

MOLOTOV

Volga River

YOSHKHAR-OLA

Vyatka River

RYE

OATS

OIL REFINERY

GORKY

CHEBOKSARY

KAZAN

Kama River

Oka River

Belaya River

UFA

MILLET

POTATOES

SARANSK

ULYANOVSK

SAW MILLS

MATCH FACTORIES

PENZA

KUIBYSHEV

ISHIMBAYEV

PAPER MILLS

WHEAT

FLOUR MILLS

URALSK

ENGELS
SARATOV

MEAT PACKING

FLOUR MILLS

WATERMELON

KAMYSHIN

Volga River

TRACTORS

K I R G H I Z

Don River

VOLGOGRAD

OIL REFINERIES

Ural River

S T E P P E

TSIMLYANSK RESERVOIR

Volga-Don Canal

FISH CANNERIES

ELISTA

ASTRAKHAN

C A S P I A N

FLOCKS OF CAMEL AND SHEEP

URAL MOUNTAINS

higher learning, including a university. Books and newspapers now appear in Mari and Mordovian languages.

On the Volga's right bank—between the Maris and the Mordovians —lies the Chuvash ASSR. About 740,000, or a little over half, of the entire Chuvash people live here.

A people of the Turkic linguistic group, the Chuvashes are akin to the Kazan Tartars, although they resented the misrule of their Tartar overlords. In 1551—a year before the conquest of the Kazan Khanate by Ivan—they seceded from it and swore allegiance to Muscovite tsars.

Cheboksary, the republic's capital, founded in 1557, is now an industrial center of 155,000 people. It specializes chiefly in machine-building, electrical, cotton textile, shoe-and-leather tanning, and food-processing industries. There are coniferous forests in the sandy areas of the country, and the newly built city of Shumerlya has a group of important modern woodworking plants.

However, Chuvashia is a predominantly agricultural country. Along the Volga's hilly bank cut by ravines there are many orchards and vegetable gardens. There is much cattle breeding in the republic. The Chuvash written language, based on the Russian alphabet, came into being in the early 1870's, half a century earlier than the Mari and the Mordovian ones.

Down the Volga, is Kazan, a large and picturesque city of 750,000, and capital of the Tartar ASSR. In street crowds, one sees many Tartar faces—swarthy, with slanting eyes and dark hair.

Kazan has long been an important intellectual center both for the Russians and the Tartars. In particular, the Kazan University, founded in 1804, has always been highly rated. It was headed for nineteen years by Nicholas Lobachevsky, a famous Russian mathematician. Among its students were Count Leo Tolstoy, the great writer, and Vladimir Lenin, creator of the Communist doctrine and of the Soviet regime.

Kazan was long an important center for buying hides and furs. Now its small old factories have been transformed into large tanning and leather-shoe concerns and into the largest Soviet pelt-dressing business. The old tallow, soap and candle works, also reconstructed, are now a leading chemical plant. Finally Kazan is noted for the production of typewriters, calculators, and other business machines. In the Tartar Republic—near Kazan—lie some of the great Volga-Ural oil fields.

Today's Tartars are descendants of Russia's former masters, inter-mingled with other peoples. There are about 5 million Tartars in Russia. Only 650,000 (47 percent of its population) of them live in the Tartar ASSR. The rest are scattered over other parts of the Soviet Union.

As Mohammedans, the Tartars had long used the Arabic alphabet for their written language. Their priests taught them literacy and the Koran. In the nineteenth century Arabic gave place to their own much simpler written language, based on the Russian alphabet. This helped the Tartars to develop their own professional class of teachers, doc-tors, and technicians much earlier than the Volga Region's other non-Russian peoples. Already in the nineteenth century there were modern Tartar poets and writers. Today there are twelve high educational establishments in Tartary. Tartars work in the Volga Region's oil industry and many others are engaged in Moscow, Kiev, or Lenin-grad as office workers, automobile mechanics, university professors, and Soviet officials.

More than half of Tartary's population is engaged in agriculture. Rye, spring wheat, potatoes, and sugar beet are grown on collective farms. Along the Volga's right bank there is a continuous string of villages, vegetable gardens, and orchards.

The fifth Volga republic, lying east of Tartary, is the Bashkir ASSR. In size it is not much larger than Arkansas. In the west, up to Belaya River, it is flat. Farther east the land rises, forming the southern Ural ranges. Forty percent of Bashkiria's territory is wooded, chiefly in these ranges. The rest is steppeland. Some of the richest Volga-Urals oil fields—Ishimbay, Tuimazy, Shkapovo—lie here. Bashkiria is also wealthy in minerals.

There are one million Bashkirs in the Soviet Union, of whom 740,000 live in the republic. Bashkiria's capital, Ufá (660,000), is a major refining center for the republic's great oil fields. It is a busy port on the Belaya River and a railway junction. Among the republic's other cities are Sterlitamak with a new soda-cement plant and synthetic rubber, glass, and food-processing industries; and Ishimbay, the "oil city."

The Bashkirs, like the Tartars, are a Turkic-speaking people of Mo-hammedan tradition, black-haired, muscular, with narrow eyes. But they are believed to be of Finnish origin, mixed with Volga Bulgars and Tartars. Most Bashkirs came under Muscovite rule in 1555–1557.

In Bashkiria one keenly feels the immediate proximity of Asia. The

Bashkirs always had been, and remained till the middle of the nineteenth century, nomadic cattle-breeders, hunters, and bee-keepers. Some of the *tarkhany*—or Bashkir aristocrats of the steppes—owned thousands of horses. For it was in horses (and sheep) that the Bashkir's wealth lay. He was hospitable, generous, warlike, lazy, and apt to plunder. In 1789 the Russian Government put the whole Bashkir people on a military footing. They had to man, equip, and permanently keep up some mounted regiments, commanded by their own chieftains. When, after Napoleon's defeat in 1814, Russian troops found themselves in Paris, the Bashkirs watered horses in the Seine River, frightening the Parisians by their "wild Asiatic look." The Bashkirs were "demilitarized" as a people only in 1865.

In the nineteenth century Bashkir lands were bought up by new settlers flocking from the outside. Nomadic cattle-breeding, requiring endless steppes for grazing, became nearly impossible. By 1900 most Bashkirs passed to settled life and agriculture, although they were poor farmers in the beginning. Now, in Bashkiria's collective farms, chiefly spring wheat and sugar beet are grown. A few of the famous Bashkir horses are still left, kept chiefly for *kumýss*, fermented mare's milk and the Bashkirs' favorite drink.

After turning south at Kazan and emerging from the Tartar ASSR, the Volga crosses, for the rest of its way to the Caspian Sea, ethnically Russian territory. Here lie the provinces of Ulyanovsk, Kuibyshev, Penza, Saratov, Volgograd, and Astrakhan.

The main cities of that part of the Volga Region are now important industrial centers. But most of them owe their early development chiefly to agriculture.

Ulyanovsk, formerly called Simbirsk, has a population of 260,000. It is here that Vladimir Lenin, whose real name was Ulyanov, was born in 1870. The house in which he grew up has been transformed into the Lenin Museum.

The region's second largest city in size (after Gorky)—and perhaps first in importance—is Kuibyshev. It is the old Samara, renamed in 1935 in honor of Valerian Kuibyshev, a noted Communist leader. It was here that the Soviet Government provisionally moved their capital in 1941, when Hitler's armies stood at the gates of Moscow.

Kuibyshev was at first a tiny fortress founded in 1586, on the Volga's left bank, in the "wild field." In the first years of this century, when railroads connected it with areas such as Siberia and Central

Asia, it became the main commercial, financial, and transshipping point on the Volga. It is now one of the fastest growing Soviet cities. It is well situated. Near it, the Volga Uplands rise, forming the picturesque Zhiguli Mountains in the "Samara Bend," and Kuibyshev sits on the river's left bank, with the mountain panorama before it, across the water.

Saratov (685,000) is the capital of the region's "black soil" belt. Before the Revolution, it was one of the main flour-milling, grain-trading, and food-processing centers in Russia. Now large engineering, chemical, and oil-refining plants have been added to it. Sitting on an elevated plateau on the Volga's right bank, it is surrounded on three sides by yellow-green mountains, which form an amphitheater around it.

A bridge joins Saratov to the city of Engels on the Volga's left bank. Before World War II Engels was the capital of the Volga German ASSR. In the eighteenth century Empress Catherine II granted to German settlers a great deal of land near Saratov, on both banks of the river. Like other small ethnical groups, the Volga Germans formed under the Soviet regime an ASSR of their own. Out of its total population of 600,000, some 400,000 were Germans.

In Imperial Russia they worked and prospered. In their area agriculture reached a much higher level than in neighboring Russian villages. The Volga Germans cooperated with the Soviet Government as well. In particular, they did not object to the collectivization of farms pressed on the country by the Communist Party.

But in August, 1941, after Nazi armies had invaded the Soviet Union, the Volga German Republic was accused of collaborating with Hitlerite Germany and was liquidated. Whether or not this was justified, scores of Volga German leaders were arrested and shot. The entire German population of the former republic was banished, scattered over wide areas of Siberia, Central Asia, and northeastern regions of European Russia.

Next along the Volga lies Volgograd (700,000). It was long known as Tsaritsyn, then, while Joseph V. Stalin was the Soviet Union's virtual dictator, it became Stalingrad. After Stalin's death in 1953, its name was changed once more, to the present Volgograd.

It is one of the region's main industrial cities, with a mammoth hydroelectric power plant operating the locks of the "Volgograd Sea," a great caterpillar tractor plant, and the "Red October" metallurgical works. These are on the Volga's right bank, on a narrow flood-plain

lying between the river and the hills, which rise in a terrace above it. On that terrace lies the well-planned city itself with its many parks.

The city played a unique role in World War II. In the summer of 1942, Hitler made an all-out attempt to deal Russia a mortal blow. He intended to take Volgograd (Stalingrad) and "cut the Volga" to prevent transporting food from the Caucasus and the Caspian area. Caucasian oil, vital to the Soviet Army and war planes would be prevented from reaching Central Russia.

A powerful German army of 330,000 men fought its way to Stalingrad. There a stubborn, seesaw battle raged for months. Every section of the city was fought over, changing hands time after time. After six months of harsh fighting, large Soviet forces were victorious. The entire besieging Nazi group of armies was trapped and surrendered.

The city had been transformed into a heap of rubble. Since then, it has been built anew. The present well-planned, neat city has three times as many buildings as before. But one large, four-story bombed-out ghost of a building, the Mill No. 4, is kept as war had left it, with a roof gutted by shells, and gaping, fire-blackened holes instead of windows. It is a "historical reservation"—a symbol of war's horror and a monument to Volgograd's heroic past.

A few miles south of the city the Volga-Don Canal begins. With its completion in 1952, Volgograd's role as a great river port and trans-shipping center was still further enhanced.

South of Volgograd the Volga flows below the ocean level. The Caspian Sea into which it drains is a landlocked sea, lying considerably below sea level. Because it evaporates more water than flows into it, it continues to dry up. Here, in the Astrakhan Province which the river crosses, the Volga's current becomes more and more sluggish, splitting into a number of side channels. Hot, dry winds blow from the southeast. Gradually, the steppe belt merges into pasture lands, sandy semi-deserts, and full deserts. There is a good deal of horned cattle and sheep breeding in the area. Patches of salt lakes and marshes are remnants of the Caspian Sea which once reached out far to the north. Some of them—such as Lake Baskunchak—supply the Soviet Union with large amounts of salt. The monotony of the landscape is relieved only by the fabulously rich melon fields, orchards, vineyards, and rice fields, wherever the soil is properly watered. East of the Volga, between Volgograd and Astrakhan, lies Kapustin Yar. It is believed to be an important testing ground for Soviet intercontinental ballistic missiles.

At the point of entering the Caspian Sea, the Volga forms a delta, about 100 miles wide, of innumerable streams, stagnant lakes, and sandbars. For centuries this has been known as one of the richest fisheries in the world. Thirty-two species of commercially valuable fish such as the caviar-producing sturgeon and beluga, the sterlet, the pike, and the herring are found in the area. Lately the Astrakhan fisheries have been considerably depleted because of poisonous industrial wastes draining into the Volga and the dams built across it.

In the Volga's estuary sits Astrakhan (population 340,000). It is situated on a number of islands joined by many bridges. Astrakhan has always housed great fish product concerns. It also has an important shipbuilding yard for fishing trawlers and for the mechanization of the fishing industry. Paper pulp is produced from reeds, for the Volga's estuary abounds in thickets of reeds.

Astrakhan is also an important transportation knot, where sea, river, and rail lines join together. Millions of tons of oil, timber, fish, salt, and cotton are yearly handled by it. It has two ports. The river port is close to the city. The sea port is a mammoth floating pier moored far off shore, at a distance of 120 miles from the city, where the sea is deep enough for large ships to dock.

The last of the Volga's autonomous ethnical units is the Kalmyk ASSR. This lies west and southwest of the Astrakhan province, in the Caspian depression. The country is a semi-desert, with salt lakes, arid in summer and cold, though almost snowless, in winter. In the south it merges into the steppes of the Northern Caucasus. In the west, Kalmyk semi-deserts pass into the Yergheni Hills, which are the last offshoots of the Volga Uplands.

The Kalmyk people—wide-faced, with narrow, slanting eyes, and a broad, flat nose—are a Mongoloid race, intermingled with Turk peoples. They speak a Mongol language and are, or were, Buddhists (Lamaists). There are 106,000 Kalmyks in the Soviet Union. Sixty-five thousand of them live in their ASSR. The rest are scattered in the Volga Region and in the Caucasus. They were always nomads and it is only in the last thirty to forty years that they have passed to settled life.

Though no longer nomads, the Kalmyks still engage chiefly in animal husbandry. On their collective farms, horned animals (for meat and dairy products), fine-fleeced sheep, and some camels are raised. Lately, Persian lamb breeding has been developed. Agriculture, though still playing a subsidiary role, is progressing, especially in the Yergheni Hills. Lately, the republic has been producing more grain than it consumes. Along the Caspian shore there is fishing. There is little industry in Kalmykia, confined to food processing and to fish canning. However, large reserves of natural gas have been discovered in the country which may bring about important changes.

Kalmykia, with a total population of over 185,000 has one city— Elista (40,000), its capital. After inhabiting felt tents for centuries, the Kalmyks now live in permanent houses resembling Russian *izby*, but built of bricks or reeds pressed with clay. Plates, forks, samovars, and teacups appeared in Kalmyk families at the beginning of our century. Today furniture has found its way into their new houses as well.

Like the Bashkirs, the Kalmyks are great *kumýss* drinkers. They are great tea drinkers, too. Virtually every meal begins with tea. But they have a way of their own of making it. They boil it with milk, butter, salt, and nutmeg.

The Kalmyks had always used the Old-Mongol written language. The new Kalmyk written language, based on the Russian alphabet, recently came into use. There are now 240 elementary and secondary, Mongol and Russian, schools in the republic. The Kalmyks have a remarkable epic (heroic) folklore dating back to at least the fifteenth century. The development of the modern Kalmyk literature and theater is encouraged and supported by Moscow.

In Kalmykia's recient past there was a tragic interlude. During World War II, in 1943, the Kalmyks—like the Volga Germans—were accused of disloyalty. Their ASSR was abolished and its entire Kalmyk population was banished to various regions in Siberia. But fourteen years later, the Communist Party and the Soviet Government made amends to them, and the people were restored to their abandoned villages.

★

THE EUROPEAN NORTH

The Soviet Union's European North, from the Gulf of Finland to the Urals, and from the Arctic Ocean to the upper Volga, is three times as large as France. But while France has 48 million inhabitants, this region has but 12 millions. Seven millions live in cities and industrial areas, chiefly along the region's seashore and its few railroads. Leningrad, "the pearl of the North," alone numbers 3.5 millions. There are concentrations of rural population in the southwestern provinces—those of Pskov, Novgorod, and Leningrad. But the rest of the immense country is empty. It has endless stretches with only two inhabitants per square mile. This is due to the region's freezing climate, for one-quarter of it lies beyond the Arctic Circle.

Near the Arctic Circle there are about 270 freezing days per year. Ice floes drift in the seas even in summer. The region's entire shore line—especially along the Gulf of Finland and the Barents Sea—is warmer than the rest of it. Inland, in the Archangel and Vologda provinces and the Komi ASSR, frosts are especially severe. In the region's north, in summer, the sun does not set at all. But in winter it never rises and the Arctic night reigns, often lit with the mysterious flames of the aurora borealis. Here is the tundra with billions of birds and pitiless mosquitoes in summer; the impenetrable coniferous *taiga* (forest), covering up to 65 percent of the territory; the nomadic

Nentsy (or Samoyeds) in sledges drawn by reindeer; numberless peat bogs and 44,000 lakes in the Karelian ASSR alone.

The area has great natural resources. The Archangel Province alone yearly yields 15 percent of all wood pulp produced in Russia. Much of the region's lumber goes south by rail, to Soviet industrial centers. Still more is floated north, in log rafts, to Archangel, at the Dvina River's estuary, for export.

During Joseph Stalin's rule (1924–53), the sawmilling and wood processing were done here by an army of convict laborers. They often were treated brutally and inhumanly. The center of the area's numerous convict labor camps was located on the Solovetsky Islands in the White Sea. Now the somber story of these camps belongs to the past.

An important role is played by very rich fisheries in the Barents Sea and in the Arctic and Atlantic oceans. The fishing fleet based in the port of Murmansk yields 20 percent of the Soviet Union's entire catch.

Especially important is the mineral wealth in the Murmansk Province, on the Kola Peninsula in the extreme northwest. The so-called Scandinavian Shield of ancient crystalline rocks reaches out here, forming the low Khibiny and Lovozersky Mountains with rough bedrock outcroppings. In recent years they have been found to contain some hundred various ores, from nickel, copper, iron ore, zirconium, and molybednum to twenty minerals which exist nowhere else in the world.

The Komi ASSR in the flat eastern part of the region also holds considerable resources. On the Izhma River there are the important Ukhta oil fields. Also found are bauxites (raw material for aluminum), and in the republic's northeastern corner, high-grade coking coal is mined in the great Vorkuta deposits. These were discovered only recently.

The Pskov, Novgorod, and Leningrad provinces form the southwestern—and comparatively warm—area of the region. In countries lying along the Baltic Sea the cold is tempered by its humid and warmer breath. Leningrad's average January temperature (18.3° F.) is higher than that of Moscow (14° F.), though it lies far north of the latter. But winter is considerably longer here than in Moscow.

Forests cover about 40 percent of the area. The rest is made up of meadows and fields. They are scattered with boulders and there are chains of morains—hills of debris deposited by glaciers that descended from Scandinavia in the Ice Age. The area is rich in swamps and lakes. Lakes Ladoga and Onega, due east of Leningrad, are the largest in Europe. In the area's rich meadows there is much cattle breeding for dairy farming and beef. Vegetables are grown for the large Leningrad market. But the land under crops is small.

It is the provinces's cities that deserve the most attention. Two of them—Pskov and Novgorod—are quite small. Pskov has some machine-building plants and flax-combing works. Novgorod engages in metal- and wood-working, food processing, and ship repairing, for it sits astride the navigable Volkhov River. Now that a natural gas pipeline from the Northern Caucasus has reached Novgorod, it is also developing large-scale chemical industries.

Many streets in both cities are unpaved, irregular, with poor, rustic houses. They would look insignificant, were it not for their many unique relics of the past. In particular, the huge walls and towers of the Novgorod kremlin, the majesty of its five-domed Cathedral of St. Sophia, the great walled Yuriev Monastery, and a number of eleventh- to fourteenth-century churches of striking originality, all these bear witness to Novgorod's remarkable historical role.

It was from Novgorod that Ryurik, the Norse chieftain, invited to assume control in 862 by Eastern Slavs, ruled. Then, as Russia's political center moved to Kiev, Novgorod became a lesser principality under it. But it lay too far from Kiev to be controlled. It virtually became a medieval republic with an elective prince.

The twelfth- to fifteenth-century Novgorod was a large and prosperous metropolis, for it took over nearly all the trade between Western Europe and Muscovy (as well as territories farther east). Sailing in heavily laden boats up the Msta River and then descending down the Volga, Novgorod merchants sold the goods brought from Western Europe in Muscovy, in Tartar regions, and in Moslem lands of the Caspian area. (Ancient Arabic coins often have been found in Novgorod.) In the West, Novgoroders traded chiefly with German cities. German ships sailed to Novgorod via the Gulf of Finland-Neva River-Lake Ladoga-Volkhov River. Fine cloth, silk, wine, products of metalworking industries were brought to Novgorod. Sable, beaver and other furs, flax, hemp, wax, train oil went to the German cities in the same holds on their return voyage.

Novgoroders gradually expanded their domains northeast, to the shores of the Barents and the White seas, and even to the Urals. They met scattered tribes and bartered with these natives, or imposed a tax on them and made them subjects of "Sovereign Great Novgorod." They founded strong points and settlements in the immense, empty land, originating some large present-day cities—Vologda, Kirov (Vyatka), Perm, Pechyora. Thus, medieval Novgorod became the first colonizer and organizer of European Russia's North.

In 1478, Great Novgorod's virtual political independence came to an end. Serious disagreements caused a rift between it and Muscovy which had become a powerful, united State. War broke out and Novgorod suffered a shattering defeat.

Grand Duke Ivan III of Moscow—talented, autocratic, ambitious— abolished the Novgorod Vyeche, its assembly of free householders or Parliament. The "liberty bell," which had summoned Novgoroders to its meetings, was exiled. So were Novgorod's boyar famlies, chief champions of its freedom. Novgorod was demoted to the status of an ordinary Muscovite city, governed by a commander of the Grand Duke.

Novgorod, its foreign trade and all its possessions—European Russia's North included—passed to Muscovy. Pskov was incorporated into the Tsardom, in a similar way, in 1510.

About 100 miles north of Novgorod are the greenish waters of the Gulf of Finland. At its eastern tip, in the Neva's estuary, sits Leningrad, the Soviet Union's second largest city (3.5 millions). The city is so far north that it is opposite the lower tip of Greenland.

Founded in 1703 by Peter the Great, the city was capital of the Russian Empire for two centuries and home of the emperors. After the Revolution in 1918, the capital was transferred back to Moscow. Until 1914, the city was called St. Petersburg; then, from 1914 to 1924, Petrograd. After Lenin's death in 1924, it was renamed for him.

Leningrad is unique. It has few rivals for beauty with its wide, straight avenues and long vistas; majestic palaces of the imperial family and noblemen's palatial homes (now both nationalized), mirrored in the steel-gray waters of the Neva's numerous side-streams and canals; granite embankments, and four hundred bridges spanning these canals.

It is flanked, on the south, by a number of small "palace cities," such as Pushkin (formerly Tsarskoye Selo), Petrodvorets (Peterhof), and Gatchina. They served as out-of-town residences of the imperial family. Some of them, with their graceful palaces, landscaped parks, gardens, pavillions, statues, lakes, fountains, are very lovely. Most palaces are now museums. In Leningrad itself, the finest museums are the immense Winter Palace, the emperors' official residence, and the adjoining Hermitage. The Winter Palace was built in 1754–62. The formal magnificance of the great state halls with inlaid parquet floors mirroring crystal chandeliers, paintings, sculptured ceilings, tall malachite vases framed in gold, give an idea of the style of the eighteenth-century Russian Court under Peter's successors. The adjoining Hermitage holds immense and invaluable art collections.

Unlike the Muscovite architecture of medieval-type kremlins and many-domed cathedrals, Leningrad's palaces are distinctly eighteenth-century European in style. The whole city reflected Peter's efforts to Europeanize Russia.

Peter realized that, due to various factors (including the Tartar Yoke), Muscovy had fallen some two centuries behind Western Europe; that instead of learning from the West, she lived in virtual isolation from it. He ordered Russian noblemen and other men of the upper classes to shave their long, traditional Muscovite beards, and to shed their Oriental-type, floor-long robes in exchange for European wigs, short *kaftans*, and stockings. He sent Russians abroad to learn foreign languages, techniques, skills, sciences, and invited European engineers, military experts, and scientists to Russia. But Europeanization required intensified trade with Europe. And that was a problem.

Profiting by Muscovy's weakness during the Time of Trouble in 1610–13, Sweden—then a mighty European power—seized a wide strip of Russian territory along the Gulf of Finland and the Neva up to Lake Ladoga. Muscovy was thus isolated from the Baltic Sea. She could trade with the West via that sea—her sole convenient trade route—only with Sweden's consent. Sweden, meanwhile, often denied it, fearing that the import of Western goods, skills, and sciences would make Muscovy too strong.

In 1700, Peter attacked Sweden. It was a long and very difficult struggle, but in two years the Russians had recaptured part of the shore of the Gulf of Finland and the Neva's banks. Peter immediately started building the city which would be Petersburg.

At this time there were only a large group of low, muddy islands. A few tiny hamlets of Russian and Karelian fishermen were scattered on them. All around was a northern wilderness of woods and swamps.

The building of a city on these islands cost untold efforts and sufferings. Year in and year out, twenty thousand Russian peasants labored here, standing to the waist in cold, liquid mud. They drove piles into the ground and dumped soil, brought in the skirt of their shirts for they had no wheelbarrows.

By 1718, European visitors described it as a "lovely city." Trade with the West via the Baltic and Russia's new capital rapidly expanded. The number of foreign merchantmen arriving in it rose from fifty-two in 1718 to four hundred and fifty in 1725 (the year of Peter's death). In the middle of the century its population was 100,000. Under Catherine the Great (1762–96), the splendor of the Court of St. Petersburg became the talk of Europe.

Petersburg was Russia's "window on Europe." Western influences rapidly awakened native Russian thought and talents. By the beginning of the nineteenth century Russia produced her first scientists, writers, and composers. Modern Russian culture—a peculiar blend of native and Western elements—was born in Petersburg.

In 1917, it was in Petersburg that the Revolution broke out, the Old Regime was overthrown and, eventually, the Bolshevik, or Communist, Party led by Lenin seized the power.

During World War II, in 1941–44, Petersburg (now Leningrad) withstood a 900-day siege by Hitler's armies. The Nazis fought their way to within five miles of its center. Only a narrow strip from Leningrad to an unoccupied stretch of Lake Ladoga's shore remained in the defenders' hands. It was their lifeline. Boats in summer and trucks driving on the lake's ice in winter brought to that strip ammunition for the city and as many supplies for its people as was possible. But not all boats or trucks got through: German bombers kept after them.

Leningraders starved. In winter, in unheated apartments, they lived in fur coats. School children wrote only in pencil, for ink froze. Epidemics broke out. And German shells kept bursting in the city. But Leningraders took it with a remarkable fortitude. They went about their daily life. They worked for Soviet fighters at the front (which was within walking distance), or joined their ranks. By the time the Nazis were driven back, 600,000 Leningraders had died. Like Stalingrad, Leningrad is rated a "hero city."

After the war, Finland, Germany's ally for the siege of the city, made minor concessions of territory to Russia along their common border. The Soviet Union received the entire northern part of the Karelian Isthmus between the Gulf of Finland and Lake Ladoga with the city and seaport of Viborg.

Leningrad holds a very important place in the country's intellectual life. It has a whole "population of scientists," scores of specialized bodies of the Soviet Academy of Sciences (especially the ones engaged in industrial research), forty institutions of higher learning, and internationally known museums, libraries, and theaters. It is also a great printing and publishing center.

Leningrad is highly industrialized with plants that produce a great variety of items. In its great shipyards, vessels of all descriptions are built. The *Lenin,* first atomic-powered icebreaker in the world, was built here.

Leningrad is also a great transportation center. Ten railways converge on it. Though no longer the unique outlet to Europe it had been under Peter the Great, Leningrad still is a great seaport. A considerable percentage of foreign trade, especially with European countries, is routed through it.

Twenty miles off Leningrad, on Kotlin Island in the Gulf of Finland, is Kronstadt. A fortress built by Peter (and repeatedly modernized) it is the main Soviet naval base in the Baltic. The Gulf is shallow here. A deep channel is kept open in it between Kronstadt and Leningrad, allowing ships of any size to reach the latter. The Gulf stays icebound from the end of November to mid-April, but the use of icebreakers considerably shortens that period.

Like Moscow, Leningrad may be called "the port of five seas." It is, primarily, the terminal of the important Volga-Baltic Inland Waterway. It was first opened for navigation in 1808. Modern requirements, however, outgrew its inadequate traffic capacity, so in 1964, the waterway was radically reconstructed. Now riverboats up to 3500 tons ply it. Bulky goods—oil, grain, Ukrainian coal—sail from the Volga to Leningrad.

Another important waterway serving Leningrad is the White Sea-Baltic Canal. Starting at Belomorsk, on the White Sea, it runs south, utilizing a number of smaller lakes in the Karelian ASSR, to the northern tip of Lake Onega. That lake connects, through other navigable bodies of water, with Leningrad.

Riding from Leningrad northeast, on a train of the Murmansk Railway, one reaches, in a few hours, the Karelian ASSR. It is a land

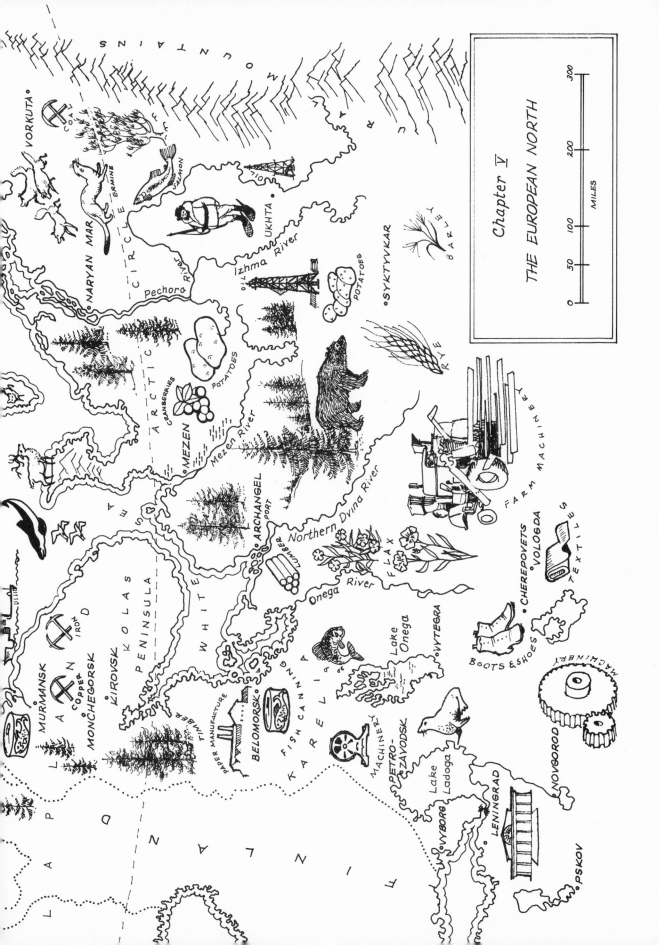

MOUNTAINS

U R A L

VORKUTA

COAL

ERMINE

SALMON

NARYAN MAR

OIL

UKHTA

ARCTIC CIRCLE

Pechora River

Izhma River

SYKTYVKAR

BARLEY

POTATOES

POTATOES

CRANBERRIES

POTATOES

MEZEN

Mezen River

RYE

ARCTIC SEA

ARCHANGEL
PORT

Northern Dvina River

FARM MACHINERY

LUMBER

FLAX

CHEREPOVETS

VOLOGDA

TEXTILES

Onega River

KOLA PENINSULA

WHITE SEA

Lake Onega

VYTEGRA

BOOTS & SHOES

MURMANSK

IRON

COPPER

KIROVSK

MONCHEGORSK

L A P L A N D

PAPER MANUFACTURE

TIMBER

BELOMORSK

KANINA

KARELIA

FISH

MACHINERY

PETRO-ZAVODSK

Lake Ladoga

MACHINERY

NOVGOROD

VYBORG

LENINGRAD

PSKOV

F I N L A N D

Chapter V

THE EUROPEAN NORTH

300

200

100

MILES

50

0

of granite, pine forests, swamps, and 44,000 lakes. Karelia is larger than the states of New York, New Jersey, and Massachusetts combined. In the north it touches on, and at places overlaps, the Arctic Circle. Its two largest lakes are Ladoga and Onega; although their southern reaches are in the Leningrad Province, most of their shoreline belongs to Karelia. The rivers are short, but swift, ample, and often ruffled by cataracts.

Winters are long here, but not very severe. In Karelia's southwest there are 120 frost-free days a year, and in its north only 90. The brown bear, retreating from the industrialized Central Russia, now lives in Karelia, as well as the wolf, the polar fox, and the lynx. Reindeer are found in the north.

The Karelians have always inhabited the country. Like the Maris and the Mordovians of the Volga Region, they are a Finno-Ugric people. There are 170,000 of them in all of the Soviet Union. But only 90,000 live in their own republic, forming 13 percent of its population. The rest of those living in the area are Russians.

The Karelians have never had a State organization or cities of their own. Trappers, fishermen, and primitive farmers growing barley, they lived by tribal order when, in the twelfth century, Novgorods colonized their land and extended their sovereignty over it. In 1478, together with Novgorod, Karelia was absorbed into the Muscovite State.

At present, the country's large-scale industries are sawmilling, wood processing, and pulp-and-paper production. Among their centers are Medvezhyegorsk and Seguezha, each with a population of under 50,000. In Petrozavodsk, the capital, there are, besides shipbuilding, fish-processing and leather-tanning plants. Another fish-processing and canning center is Belomorsk, terminal of the White Sea—Baltic Canal. Fishing plays an increasing role in the republic.

Karelia's main agricultural area lies between Lakes Ladoga and Onega. Barley, vegetables, and especially potatoes are grown. Cattle breeding is another occupation. Karelian peasants live in *izby* very like the Russian ones.

The Karelians have a rich spoken tradition, but to this day they have no written language of their own. The difference between their southern and northern dialects is too great for a common literary language. Russian and Finnish are used as official languages in Karelia's institutions with instruction in Karelia's schools, as well as in the university, conducted in Russian.

The Murmansk Province, occupying the Kola Peninsula, is north of Karelia. Almost all of it lies beyond the Arctic Circle. The western part of the Barents Sea is warmed by the Gulf Stream. Though ice floes appear in it in the fall, it does not freeze, and it warms the north of the Kola Peninsula. The average January temperature of Murmansk is one degree higher than that of Leningrad, which lies a good deal to the south.

The Kola Peninsula is described as "a land of darkness and eternal gloom." During the Arctic night, oblique, pink sunrays play for an hour a day only on snow-covered mountains and hills. Over the tundra, swamps, and lakes of the peninsula's flat, endless eastern section, complete darkness reigns.

Murmansk, the province's main city (population 272,000), is the largest Arctic city in the world. It lies at the head of the Kola Bay (or Fjord) cutting deep into the peninsula, and near the mouth of the Tuloma River. Murmansk is a great seaport, center of the fishing industry, and the main base of the large Soviet Arctic fleet of fishing trawlers. Beside their "native" sea these boats also operate far afield— off the shores of Greenland, Iceland, and Newfoundland. Murmansk also has various related industries, such as ship repairing, fish canning, and tin can production. It also has a College of Navigation and an Arctic Research Institute for Ichthyology and Oceanography. It is a modern city with electricity, boulevards, cinemas, theaters, yet it is only fifty years old.

The Kola Peninsula has been Russian since the twelfth to fourteenth centuries, when the Novgoroders had colonized it. But until 1916 the huge peninsula was virtually empty. The great change began during World War I (1914–18). Imperial Russia was in need of a constant flow of war supplies from her Western Allies. The Baltic and the Black Seas were blockaded, respectively, by Germany and Turkey. Archangel, the large White Seaport, was frozen in for five or six months a year. The Russian Government built the Murmansk Railway, connecting St. Petersburg with the ice-free Kola Bay. Despite great engineering difficulties, it was ready and began to function in 1916. At that time Murmansk's population was about one thousand. Barents Sea fisheries and shipping possibilities enabled it to expand 272 times in fifty years.

The Murmansk Railway opened up the roadless Kola Peninsula. From 1921 on, the Soviet Academy of Sciences explored the geological resources of the Khibiny and Lovozersky Mountains east of Lake

Imandra and of elevations west of it, in the center of the peninsula. The geologists discovered great apatite-nephelite deposits. Mining boom towns mushroomed up in the area. One of them, Kirovsk, born only in 1930 in rocky hills in the midst of apatite mines, now has a population of 50,000. Another, Monchegorsk, which is a copper and nickel mining center, has outgrown that figure. Hydroelectric power plants sprang up in the country. There are also important mineral deposits elsewhere in the province. In particular, in its northwestern corner, near the sixteenth-century Russian fishing village of Pechengá, large quantities of nickel are mined.

The peninsula's total population has now increased to about 700,000. And, apparently, this is only the beginning of its development.

Some of the province's inhabitants are Russian Pomors (*pomóry*), or tall, blond, husky descendants of the Novgoroders who had settled along its shores. They were known as daring and experienced men who ventured out to sea, in their small flat-bottomed boats, in any storms. Now many of them are crew members on fishing trawlers, workers at the Murmansk canning combinat, or miners. There are also newcomers from all parts of the Soviet Union in the province; and former inmates of northern convict labor camps, who are now staying on in the country.

Some 1,800 *Saamy* (Lapps) still live in the province. They are the same, almost extinct, Lapps of the Finno-Ugric stock as those in

Northern Scandinavia, the original inhabitants of these regions. Until quite recently, Kola Lapps were nomads. Along with fishing in lakes, and hunting, the main source of their livelihood were the reindeer. The Lapps ate the animal's meat, wore its pelt, used it for bedding, and rode in the reindeer-drawn sledge. In winter they grazed their animals in wooded, mountainous central areas around Lake Lovozero. In summer they drove them across the peninsula's tundras, toward the sea. Here, winds kept away clouds of mosquitoes, which elsewhere drove the animals crazy.

But by 1940 the Lapps were settled on collective fishing and reindeer-breeding farms, organized with the Communist Party's prompting. There the Lapps have—or so we are told—schools, hospitals, and new houses (instead of their old huts with a hole in the roof for a chimney).

In the province there is some dairy farming and, near the larger cities, vegetable growing. Experimentation is carried on with some cereals. But there the province's agriculture ends. The country is too sunless and cold, and its soil too poor, for much produce. There are blue fox- and mink-breeding collective farms; and there is quite a bit of reindeer breeding—not by the Lapps alone.

By far the largest part of the Soviet Union's Northern European Region is made up of the provinces of Archangel and Vologda and the Komi ASSR. Here, too, are the islands of the White, the Barents, and the Kara seas—Solovki (or Solovetsky Islands), Kolguyev, Novaya Zemlya, Vaigach, and Franz Josef Land, all falling within the jurisdiction of the Archangel Province.

The bulk of the immense territory (except for its tundra belt and the islands), is covered with dense woods, and is the kingdom of the timber industry. The greater part of the timber is exported abroad. Logs are rafted and floated on the four great rivers of the region—the Onega, the Northern Dvina, the Mezen, and the Pechyora—to the seaports at their estuaries. These timber industry ports are Onega, Archangel, Mezen, and Naryan-Mar. Here, in summer, logs are piled in endless rows along the waterfront—especially at Archangel, where the Dvina, in its estuary, splits into several streams. All through the winter sawmills work to transform logs into lumber. In Archangel, which is by far the largest of these cities, there are twenty sawmills with well over one hundred saw-frames, plus two paper-and-pulp combinats, and a wood chemicals plant. In spring, with the resumption of navigation in the White Sea, lumber is shipped abroad. A good deal of sawmilling and wood processing is done in various small centers, not only along the rivers, but also along the Archangel to Moscow and Vorkuta to Konosha Railways. From thence timber or processed wood go by rail to various domestic destinations. It is natural that the life of the Northern Region is attuned to the timber industry and largely determined by it.

Archangel is an important seaport, industrial center, and the largest city of the entire region after Leningrad. It is also, like Murmansk, an important base of the Soviet fishing fleet in Arctic waters. The White Sea is also rich in fish—although not quite so rich as the Barents Sea. It has ship-repairing yards, factories processing the catch of sea animals, and food-industry concerns. It is an important cultural center for the north.

The city is scattered, on both banks of the Dvina and on the islands in its estuary, over dozens of miles, forming a mass of "smart" blocks, fishing villages, industrial centers, workmen's settlements. During these ten years, west of Archangel, its "satellite," Severodvinsk, has grown up.

Archangel's origins are unusual for a Russian city. In 1553, an expedition of three ships, commanded by Sir Hugh Willoughby, sailed from Deptford, England, seeking for a northern sea passage to Cathay, or China. During the winter Sir Hugh and the crew of two of the ships perished "from want of experience to have made caves and stoves." But the third ship, *Edward Bonaventure*, with Richard Chancellor as captain, drifted into the White Sea. There it dropped anchor at the mouth of the Northern Dvina, near Archangel Michael's Monastery.

Chancellor was taken to Moscow. He delivered a letter from King Edward VI to Ivan the Terrible. The Tsar received him very graciously, amidst great splendor, and granted important trade privileges to the English.

Soon a city, named Archangel in 1613, grew up where Chancellor had landed. And it was by the "northern route," around Scandinavia, that Muscovy's trade with Europe proceeded for the next 150 years. This lent Archangel a considerable importance.

But the route was costly, slow, hazardous. Ten sailing ships—for such was an average fleet sent from England—could make the round trip no more than once a year, carrying to Archangel, and bringing back, a total of about 1,200 tons.

With the birth of Petersburg, Archangel declined. Even as late as 1900, it remained a small, provincial city with a population of 22,000. It is only with the immense development of the timber industry, and with the growth of the importance of Northern fisheries, that it has assumed its present proportions (300,000 inhabitants) and role.

Northeast of Archangel, forming a wide belt along the White and the Barents Seas, lies a large tundra. It is as flat as a desk, except for the Timan Ridge of hills running north to south in the middle of it and separating the drainage basins of the Northern Dvina from that of the Pechyora. A large part of that tundra including the seashore, though remaining within the jurisdiction of the Archangel Province, is segregated into the Nenets National District. The Nenets are also a Finnish people, but of a separate, Samodian group. Formerly they were known as *Samoyeds*. There are about 17,000 of them in their sparsely-peopled national district, whose capital is the port of Naryan-Mar (13,000). Fishermen, hunters, reindeer-breeders, most Nenetsy still are nomads. Some of them go into the timber industry. Besides those living in the district, another 8,000 of them are scattered in Siberia.

The Soviet islands in the Arctic seas surrounding Archangel Province are a scene of northern desolation, except for the Solovki. One-quarter of the surface of Novaya Zemlya, for instance, permanently remains under a thick layer of ice; the remaining three-quarters emerge from under the ice cover in summer only to reveal the tree-less tundra. It is rocky, with fjords cutting deep into the shore line. There are seals, walruses, lemmings, polar foxes, reindeer, and white bears. Novaya Zemlya is huge, equal in length to the distance from New York to Florida and about as wide as Florida. Until 1869, when Feodor Vylka, a Nenets, settled on it, no one lived there at all. Only in 1910 did the first permanent settlement appear on it. Today it numbers about 550 inhabitants, mainly Nenetsy.

However, there have been meteorological and other scientific stations on these islands for a long time. In the years of the Soviet regime their number greatly increased. Also on the islands are intermediary bases of the Northern Sea Route, which the Soviet Government began in 1932.

Navigators and scientists long dreamed of finding a through passage to the Orient around the northern shores of Siberia. The Russians believed that a sea route from Archangel (or Murmansk) to the Russian Far East, in particular to Vladivostok, would greatly help in the development of the potentially rich Northern Siberia. That part of Siberia is very difficult to reach overland, from Siberia's inhabited and developed southern belt.

Before 1932, only three navigators succeeded in negotiating the Northern Sea Passage from end to end. This was, however, but a partial success, for each one of them had to spend the winter on the way, his ship immobilized by ice. This would obviously not make the route valuable for supplying Northern Siberia's isolated settlements.

In 1932, an expedition headed by Otto Schmidt, a noted Russian scientist and Arctic explorer, set out from Archangel aboard the ice-breaker *Sibiryakov* for Vladivostok. Schmidt successfully negotiated nearly all of the way around Sibera and, before reaching the Bering Straits, was crossing the Chukotsk Sea, already filled with ice floes. Then early one morning the crew heard a terrific blow; the *Sibiryakov* shook violently and stopped. Its propeller was broken by ice and went to the bottom. The crew broke the ice that formed about the ship by setting off explosions, put up the sails, and thus managed to reach the Bering Strait and the Pacific. Thus the *Sibiryakov* was the first ship to have covered all of the Northern Sea Route in one season.

Two years later the icebreaker *Litke* successfully sailed from one end of the Northern Sea Route to the other. And in 1935, the first caravan of freighters accompanied by icebreakers sailed the entire way without mishap.

Now it is an established sea route equipped with powerful ice-breakers, lighthouses, fueling and meteorological stations and ports. The trip lasts 70 to 120 days, usually from June to October. The route serves to export lumber and coal from Siberia. From European Russia, and from Vladivostok in the East, by the Northern Sea Route to settlements and new ports along the endless North Siberian shore go flour, cattle, machines, books, and consumer goods.

Among the cities of the Archangel and Vologda provinces, Vologda (160,000) is the most notable. It is an important railway center; the Archangel-Moscow, the Vorkuta-Leningrad, and the Vologda-Sverdlovsk (Siberia) lines meet here. Near Vologda the Sukhona River, a tributary of the Northern Dvina, is joined by a canal to the reservoir of Cherepovets, which is a link of the Volga-Baltic Waterway. Vologda engages in wood processing, metalworking, and textile industries. An ancient and attractive city, begun the same year as Moscow (1147), it has preserved some remarkable sixteenth- to eighteenth-century architectural monuments. Important, too, is Kotlas, in the south of the Archangel Province. Besides being a ship-repairing, sawmilling, and paper-and-pulp producing center, it is the crossing of three railway lines and three rivers.

Four percent of the area in these provinces is under the plow, most of it in the Vologda Province, and flax and barley are grown. In the intensely green water-meadows along the Northern Dvina and its tributaries, there is a great deal of reindeer and dairy-cattle breeding. The Kholmogory cows, bred in the area of the Archangel province of that name, are among the finest in Russia.

The Russian natives of the Archangel and Vologda provinces are tall, blond, sturdy. The early Novgorod colonizers of that wide area were joined, from the thirteenth and fourteenth centuries on, by colonizers coming from Muscovy. People fled here from the Tartar Yoke. Monasteries carved out huge estates for themselves in these endless woods. Fugitive serfs and persecuted religious "schismatics" also sought refuge in this area.

These people settled in small villages along the rivers. They lived in seclusion. Some villages remained out of touch for years with what was going on in Russia's nerve centers. Thus they preserved intact many of the old songs, fairy tales, and epic poems of the Russian folklore, which were transmitted orally from generation to generation. Russian scholars in Moscow and Petersburg have carefully collected that rich heritage of the past.

Although the Komi ASSR is larger than Finland, it has a population of only 950,000. A little over 30 percent of them are Komis, formerly known as Zyrians; like many other non-Russian peoples of the Soviet Union, they are Finno-Ugrics.

The Komis have long been a settled people. Hunting squirrel, fox, marten, ermine, elk, bear—sometimes with an old firelock—still plays an important role. In some areas the *voer kerkas,* or small one-room hunters' log cabins with a fireplace, still exist where any hunter may find refuge from the severe cold. In the southern areas of the republic agriculture has been more important for a long time. With the collectivization of farms by the Soviets, the primitive wooden plow has given place to modern agricultural machinery. Rye, barley, and potatoes are the cultures grown. The chief means of transportation are the boat, the horse and, in the north, the reindoor; also, for longer distances, the airplane. Reindeer-breeding, incidentally, has been steadily developing.

The growth of the large-scale timber industry, of the Vorkuta coal mines, and of the Ukhta oil fields, as well as the construction (in 1941) of the Kotlas-Vorkuta railway, have been increasingly drawing the Komis into industry and into the general Soviet economic life. In

Syktyvkar (90,000), the republic's villagelike capital, the industries are shipbuilding, leather tanning, wood and food processing.

Culturally, the Komi ASSR has been making a steady progress since the end of the nineteenth century. By 1914, about half of school-age children were receiving education. Now school education is universal. The first written language had been devised for the Komis by an outstanding Russian churchman, Bishop Stefan, who preached Christianity to them in the fourteenth century. The bishop's language, however, did not take hold. Finally a Komi written language based on the Russian alphabet was worked out and came into use. Now, there are several institutions of higher learning and there are Komi fiction writers, Komi playwrights, and a Komi theater.

6

★

THE WEST:
BALTIC REPUBLICS,
KALININGRAD, BELORUSSIA

THE BALTIC REPUBLICS: ESTONIA, LATVIA, LITHUANIA

Estonia, Latvia, and Lithuania combined are not as large as the state of Kansas, and their combined population is only 6,300,000 (Estonia: 1,200,000; Latvia: 2,200,000; and Lithuania: 2,900,000). They are Union republics; they have—at least in principle—the same status as the immense RSFSR. This means—again, in principle—that they remain members of the Soviet Union only as long as they wish; should they prefer to secede from it, they could do so.

Estonians form 74 percent, Letts (native inhabitants of Latvia) 62 percent, and Lithuanians 80 percent of the population of their respective lands and they have always lived there. Estonians speak a Finno-Ugric language. But the Lettish and the Lithuanian tongues form a separate Baltic group of Indo-European languages, which are closer to the Slavic ones than any other language.

All three republics border on the Baltic Sea or its gulfs. West of the Leningrad Province, the Gulf of Finland washes the northern shore of the Estonian Republic. It is a rugged shore, indented by numerous fjords and natural harbors. Some distance inland, a formation of hard limestone rises in a steep, almost vertical escarpment, up to 450 feet in height, which the Russians call the *Glint*. Now running close to the shore, now receding from it, the Glint penetrates deep into the Leningrad Province. In the west, where the Gulf joins the Baltic Sea, the escarpment breaks up, forming an archipelago of the Moonsund Islands, four of which are comparatively large.

The shore turns south, forming the Gulf of Riga, then bordering the Baltic Sea itself, it straightens, losing its indentations. Here it is marked by low, sandy dunes, often overgrown with pine forests. The dunes (and, in Estonia, the Glint) often obstruct the drainage of the country, rich in marshlands and lakes. The main rivers of the region are the Narva (Estonia), the Western Dvina (Latvia), and the Neman (Lithuania).

The area's Baltic climate is humid and temperate. Winters and summers are mild. Along the shore, the average January temperature is 25° F. to 35° F. Rivers are covered with ice for three to four months. The Baltic itself does not freeze at all. The Gulfs of Finland and of Riga freeze along the shores, but only for a short time. Ice remains thin; lanes are easily cleared through it by icebreakers. Thus, during the early winter months, Tallin, Estonia's main port, automatically takes over the functions of icebound Leningrad.

Though the region lies in the belt of mixed forests, only 25 percent of it remains wooded. Its acid, grayish soil, strewn with boulders, is not particularly fertile. In places, the reclamation of swampy areas is very expensive. Rain often interferes with the harvesting of crops. Therefore, in Estonia, only 18 percent of land is under cultivation; in Latvia over 25 percent; in Lithuania the figure rises to 40 percent. Rye, potatoes, flax, vegetables and—on better fertilized lands—sugar beets are grown. The region has excellent pastures, and there is much dairying and pig raising. Lakes are used for fish hatcheries and fishing.

The Baltic Region is not rich in mineral resources. Deposits of oil shale in Estonia, near Narva, overlapping into the Leningrad Province, are the main ones. There are, also in Estonia, phosphorite deposits (used for fertilizers). Various building materials are to be found in different localities. There is a good deal of peat, on which a number of electric power plants are run. On the larger rivers, there are hydroelectric power plants.

Estonian and Latvian tribes never evolved an early State of their own. In the thirteenth century, part of their land was conquered by Denmark, then all of it by the Germans, and later by the Swedes. In

1700–21, Peter the Great wrested the country from Sweden and incorporated it into Russia.

All the while, Estonians and Letts formed the lower or peasant class in their own land. They were serfs of predominantly German noblemen. (Serfdom was abolished in these Baltic lands by the Russian Government in 1817.) In Baltic cities, too, economic power was in the hands of German burghers. Baltic peasants—poor and for the most part landless even after the emancipation—strongly resented their German squires. It was only in the 1870's that they were gradually able to redeem the holdings which they farmed for their former masters.

But German cultural influence was and perhaps still remains strong in the region. Estonians and Letts have the reputation of being orderly, sturdy, very hard-working. An overwhelming majority of them belong, or did until recently, to the Lutheran Church.

The Lithuanians, on the contrary, developed in the thirteenth century an independent and powerful State of their own—the Grand Duchy of Lithuania. It rapidly expanded: the princes of the western Russian lands willingly joined it, seeking protection from the Tartar Yoke. By 1460, Lithuania contained important Russian principalities—those of Polotsk, Vitebsk, Smolensk, Kiev, and others, or all of today's Belorussia and much of the Ukraine. It reached from the Baltic to the Black Sea.

Then Lithuania fell under a strong Polish influence. The two countries were even united into one State. But by the eighteenth century the Polish-Lithuanian Kingdom virtually collapsed and was divided by Russia, Prussia, and Austria. As a result of its three consecutive partitions (1773–95), not only Belorussian and Ukrainian lands were restored to the Russian Empire, but it also received Lithuania proper.

Thus, after 1795, all three Baltic countries found themselves under the Russian rule.

The Baltic area's early economic development was helped by the proximity of St. Petersburg. From the 1860's on, railways linked Russia's main economic regions to Baltic ports—Reval (now Tallin), Riga, Libau (Liepaja). As a result, Estonia and Latvia quickly became industrialized. Shipbuilding, railroad car construction, electrical, textile and chemical (chiefly rubber) industries grew up. Lithuania remained a less industrialized, but more agriculturally important area.

In the early stage of the Soviet Revolution with its chaos, civil wars, famines, the three Baltic countries seceded from Russia and—with

British and French aid—became, in 1918, independent republics. But they remained independent for only twenty-two years.

When World War II broke out, but before the Soviet Union was brought into it, the Soviet Government demanded and received from the governments of the Baltic States the right to occupy, as a measure of "mutual security," land, naval, and air bases on their territory. Soviet Army units marched into the Baltic lands, which found themselves at Moscow's mercy. In 1940, under strong Soviet pressure, the Baltic Governments organized Parliamentary elections in which no "capitalist" parties were allowed to nominate candidates. Thus, Estonian, Latvian, and Lithuanian Communists—or pro-Communists—alone were returned to the three respective Parliaments. Then, on the request of these Parliaments, the three Baltic countries were incorporated into the Soviet Union as SSR's. This act has not been recognized by the United States.

Soviet statisticians hold that, after World War II, a great industrial progress has been achieved in the Baltic Region. For now that the three republics form part of the huge Soviet economic system, market for their industrial production is always guaranteed—as is, also, access to the raw materials needed. Therefore, quite a few new industries have grown up in the region, or old ones have been reequipped and expanded. These include the production of various machinery, fertilizer, and instruments. By 1963, the Baltic Republics' total industrial production had increased to fourteen times that of 1940.

Each of the Baltic Republics has a cultural life of its own. In these twenty-odd years the educational facilities in the region have greatly increased. Each Baltic land has radio broadcasts and television programs in its own tongue. A number of newspapers, magazines, novels, plays, and books of various other types are published in Estonian, Latvian, and Lithuanian. In the Baltic Region, just as anywhere else in the Soviet Union, education and cultural life are Communist-controlled. Baltic seaside resorts attract a great many Soviet vacationers.

Of the region's cities, Tallin (322,000), Estonia's capital, is probably the most attractive, though not the largest. It is the seat of Estonia's government and the center of its culural life.

Tallin is located at the head of a fjord which cuts deep inland. The city grew up around the fourteenth-century castle with great fortress walls and the tall Long Hermann tower sitting high on a crag. Beside it sits a modern cathedral with five gilded domes. From this elevation one sees the old city around the castle; the belt of modern and brand-new housing developments and factories farther out; and, finally, the sea with its golden beaches. The old city is striking. The spires of its ancient churches (the oldest dating back to 1240); medieval, gabled houses with high Gothic roofs; narrow winding streets all make it look like an old German or Danish city rather than a Soviet one.

Most of Estonia's heavy industry is located in Tallin. Besides this it produces textile goods, house furniture, musical instruments, and has a large fish-canning plant. It is an important seaport as well.

Tartu owes its claim to distinction to its fine university founded in 1802. It also engages in agricultural machine-building, furniture-making, and food processing. The city lies in the east, where both Estonian and Russian tribes lived in early centuries. Formerly it was called Yuriev.

Riga (660,000), is not only Latvia's capital but also the largest city and economic center of the entire Baltic Region. The bulk of Latvia's machine-building, instrument-making, chemical, consumer, and food-processing industries are concentrated here. Riga is also a powerful transport tand transshipping center.

Riga sprawls on both banks of the broad Western Dvina near the place where it pours into the Gulf of Riga. Like Tallin, it has a remark-able old section, with spired Gothic churches, the yellow walls of the castle, an Assembly Hall of medieval guilds and orders of Baltic

chivalry, and gabled houses with pointed roofs. Riga is the seat of the Latvian Academy of Sciences and of nearly all institutions of higher learning in the country.

The life of Latvia's western part is closely linked up with the sea. Among the cities of that area the most important are Ventspils and Liepaja. Both are ice-free ports on the Baltic Sea proper.

Vilnius, Lithuania's ancient capital, first mentioned in the documents of the twelfth century, has about 300,000 inhabitants. Ruins of Grand Duke Gedymin's fourteenth-century castle still survive on the city's Castle Hill, and one of its towers has been restored by Lithuania's present government. The city is on the Vilya, a tributary of Neman River, and is surrounded by picturesque hills.

Vilnius had little industry other than small food-processing and consumer industries' concerns. Lately machinery construction plants, as well as large shoe and clothes factories, have been added. The city lies at the crossing of important railways.

Another sizeable ancient Lithuanian city is Kaunas, formerly called Kovno. Situated at the confluence of the Neman and the Vilya and astride two important railways, it is also a transport center. It engages in silk, wool, food-processing, furniture-making, match, and pulp-and-paper industries.

Finally Klaipeda (formerly Memel) is Lithuania's only seaport—and an important one. It has ship repair facilities, and it specializes in the construction of port equipment, as well as in fish-canning, wood-processing, and cotton textile industries. Pelanga, a few miles north of Klaipeda, is one of the most popular seaside resorts in the region.

THE KALININGRAD PROVINCE

In 1945, in accordance with a decision taken at the Potsdam Conference by the heads of the three main Allied States (the USA, Britain, and the USSR), Eastern Prussia was taken away from the defeated Germany and partitioned between Poland and the Soviet Union. Its southern half went to the former, and the northern half, with the city, port, and naval fortress of Koenigsberg, to the latter. Koenigsburg has been renamed Kaliningrad, after Michael Kalinin, President of the Soviet Union for many years. Although the only Soviet land on which the Kaliningrad area borders is the Lithuanian SSR, it has been made an administrative province not of that SSR, but of the RSFSR, or Russia proper.

That province is a little larger than the state of Connecticut. Upon East Prussia's partition, the great bulk of its German population was expelled and went to the remaining parts of Germany. The Kaliningrad Province was resettled with Soviet citizens—chiefly Great Russians from overpopulated regions. The Soviet Government offered the new settlers free transportation and housing. In the last stage of World War II most of the province's cities and rural settlements suffered much destruction. Since then, they have been rebuilt by the Soviet authorities, or with their help. At present, the province has over 680,000 inhabitants. Two-thirds of them are engaged in industry, transportation services, and fishing, and one-third in agriculture.

Fishing has an important place. The country's natural resources are confined to peat (which is plentiful), various building materials, and amber. The yellowish translucent amber, with "smoky clouds" inside, is highly valued for cigarette holders, beads, and other ornaments, and for use in the chemical industry. It is mined along the seashore.

Kaliningrad has a population of 253,000. The city sits astride the navigable Pregolia (Pregel) River, four and a half miles from its mouth in a shallow gulf separated from the open sea by a long sand bar. For ships needing up to twenty feet of water, access to the city is secured by an artificial canal kept open in the gulf.

The city is economically important. It produces automobile spare parts, railroad rolling stock, and port and fishing trawlers' equipment. It has food-processing, wood-processing, and pulp-and-paper industries (using chiefly wood imported from other Soviet regions). Kaliningrad is also one of the main bases of the Soviet fishing fleet in the Baltic, which yields large catches of sprat, eel, and cod. The trawlers also venture out for herring into the North Sea and into the Atlantic, as far as Newfoundland.

Founded in 1255 by the Teutonic Order, Koenigsberg was, for a time, the seat of the grand dukes of Prussia, but after World War II few monuments of that age remain.

Of the smaller cities of the province, Sovietsk—formerly called Tilsit—on the Neman, witnessed a historical event. In 1807, two mighty enemies, Emperors Napoleon I of France and Alexander I of Russia, met here to make peace. A raft was moored in the middle of the Neman—with French troops aligned on its left bank, the Russians on its right bank. A beautiful pavilion was pitched on the raft. Napoleon and Alexander rowed to the raft, entered the pavilion, then emerged as friends in two hours: the Tilsit Treaties of Peace and of Alliance were worked out. Yet, five years later, Napoleon led the French Army on Moscow, the beginning of the end of his domination over Europe.

BELORUSSIA

The Belorussian SSR, which is a little larger than Nebraska, lies south and southeast of the Baltic Republics. It forms an irregular triangle bordering in the west on Poland, and in the east on the Central Industrial Region. Belorussia is one of the two Soviet republics (the other being the Ukraine) which, besides being represented in the United Nations as parts of the USSR, are also members of the UN as individuals.

Belorussia's total population is 8.5 millions. It is a comparatively densely peopled part of the Soviet Union, with 120 inhabitants per square mile. Eighty-one percent of its population are Belorussians (or White Russians) who have always dwelt here. The remaining people are Great Russians, Poles, Jews, and Ukrainians.

Originally all Russians spoke the same language. However, the Belorussians developed a tongue of their own, probably when it was part of the Grand Duchy of Lithuania—and later of the Polish- Lithuanian Kingdom—from the fourteenth to the end of the eighteenth century. After this it was reunited with the rest of Russia. Later, however, from 1921 to 1939, the western quarter of Belorussia's territory, including the cities of Pinsk, Baranovichi, Brest, Grodno, Molodechno, again belonged to Poland.

Before the Revolution of 1917, Belorussia was regarded as one of Russia's poor and backward agricultural regions, due both to geographical factors and its position as a pathway for ambitious aggressors who had marched on Moscow—from Charles XII of Sweden in 1708 to Hitler in the 1940's.

Belorussia's recovery after the Nazi devastation was remarkably swift. By 1963, according to Soviet statistics, its industrial production already exceeded the pre-war level by 580 percent.

Tempered by Baltic winds, Belorussia's climate is milder than that of the Central Industrial Region, although the two lie on the same parallel.

About one-third of Belorussia's territory consists of woods, one-third of swamps, and the rest is arable land. Such a lack of workable

BALTIC SEA

GULF OF RIGA

TALLIN

RADIOS

MUSICAL INSTRUMENTS

TEXTILE MILLS NARVA

ESTONIA S.S.R.

Lake Peipsi

TARTU

CHEMICAL INDUSTRY

AGRICULTURAL MACHINERY

Lake Pskov

LIEPAJA

SAND DUNES

RIGA

LEATHER GOODS

WOOD AND PAPER MILLS

LATVIA S.S.R.

SHIPYARDS

KLAIPEDA

FISH CANNERIES

TEXTILES

KALININGRAD
KALININGRAD TILSIT

LITHUANIA S.S.R.

POTATOES

FLAX

OATS

Dvina River

FURNITURE

RYE

KAUNAS

FOOD PROCESSING

VILNIUS

CLOTHING MANUFACTURE

RYE

SALMON

POLOTSK

FLAX

CHEMICAL PLANT

VITEBSK

BELOVEZHSKAYA FOREST

GRODNO

Neman River

BEREZINA CANAL

MINSK

P O L A N D

HERD OF WILD BISON

SLONIM

BARANOVICHI

BELORUSSIA S.S.R.

Berezina River

MOGHILEV

ROLLING STOCK

POTATOES

TOOLS

Sozh River

BREST

Bug River

WHEAT

HONEY

TOBACCO

OIL REFINERY

MOZYR

Pripyat River

River

GOMEL

Dnieper River

WOODWORKING

Chapter VI

THE BALTIC REPUBLICS, KALININGRAD, BELORUSSIA

0   30   100   150   200
MILES

land in a predominantly agricultural country has always been Belorussia's misfortune.

North of its center, Belorussia is bisected from southwest to northeast by the Belorussian Ridge. East of the republic, this joins the Smolensk-Moscow Ridge. It is a wide belt (formed by a moraine marking the southern limit of the latest glaciation) of softly rising hills and flat-topped elevations. The highest peak, lying west of Minsk, Belorussia's capital, is 1200 feet.

North of the Ridge is an undulating lake country, similar to southern Lithuania. To the south the Ridge gives way to a wide plain which passes into a huge depression along the course of the Pripyat River, a navigable tributary of the Dnieper. The Pripyat splits into numberless streams for almost 250 or more miles, forming a whole swamp country known as Polesye (Woodlands)—a sort of Russian Everglades.

Belorussia is almost as rich in rivers as it is in swamps; the Belorussian Ridge divides those belonging to the northern (Baltic) and the southern (Black Sea) drainage basins. The Western Dvina, the Neman, and the Western Bug flow north; the Dnieper (rising in the province of Smolensk) and its tributaries, the Berezina, the Pripyat, the Sozh, flow south.

Rolling or flat terrain; mixed woods of pine, spruce, oak, birch, alder, and aspen; fields covered with little, greenish-blue flowers of flax (one of Belorussia's main crops); a river with marshy banks—such is the prevailing Belorussian landscape.

Belorussian woods are rich in fur-bearing animals, including the brown bear and the valuable beaver. The republic's woods are rich, too, in birds, fruit, berries, and a great variety of edible mushrooms. These "gifts of the forest" have always played a part in the country's life. Near the Polish frontier lies the famous *Belovezhskaya Pushcha* (*pushcha* means virgin forest), which was the Tsar's own hunting ground. Now it is a national reservation. Animals virtually extinct elsewhere in Europe, such as the aurochs resembling the American bison, still live here in carefully guarded freedom.

The main agricultural areas lie on the Belorussian Ridge and in the east of the country. With flax (accounting for 20 percent of the Soviet Union's flax fiber), rye and potatoes are the main crops. Wheat fields are found in the south and center. In the provinces of Gomel, Grodno, and Minsk tobacco is grown, and in the latter two provinces, beets. Areas around the republic's main cities, such as Minsk, Grodno, Vitebsk, and Moghilev, specialize in vegetable gardening and horticulture. Cattle and pigs are raised everywhere, and Belorussia also produces a considerable amount of honey.

To increase the acreage of arable lands, drainage is being energetically pushed on by the Belorussian Government, especially in Polesye. Trench excavators at work are a usual sight. By 1963 an area equal to one-sixth of the present square mileage of Belorussia's swamps was reclaimed.

Until recently, peat was regarded as Belorussia's chief industrial asset, for it serves as fuel for the country's power plants and as a fertilizer. Deposits of potassium and rock salts, used for chemical fertilizer industry, have been discovered in the south. Far more important is the discovery of oil and large deposits of oil shales recently found in the Pripyat depression in the Mozy area.

In the last twenty years the country has been greatly industrialized. A number of large machine and machine-tool building plants, chemical and other modern concerns have grown up and their products are used all over the Soviet Union. Recently, Belorussia's power facilities have been unified into a single grid. The percentage of city dwellers in Belorussia's population increased from 14 in 1913 to 37 in 1964.

Minsk, the republic's capital, sits on an undulating terrain astride the little Svisloch River. The city dates from 1067 when it was the crossing point of important trade routes between Russian principalities and their western neighbors.

In the nineteenth century it was a dusty, provincial administrative center. Soon afterward two important railways passed through the city and breathed new life into it. Then, in 1945, it was turned to rubble by the retreating Nazi. The Germans destroyed virtually all the Belorussian cities.

Today Minsk is virtually a new city; much of it has been redesigned; its wide boulevards, squares, and streets are bordered by modern buildings and apartment blocks. Its population is 717,000, and it is now an important industrial center, the headquarters of Belorussia's cultural life.

In Belorussia's northermost corner, on the Western Dvina, is the ancient city of Polotsk. During the tenth to thirteenth centuries it was the largest Russian principality in the region. Today it is a tiny provincial city with a new silk-fiber plant and a large oil refinery which serve the entire Belorussia.

Southeast of Polotsk, also on the Dvina, is Vitebsk on both banks of the river. An ancient city, it is now one of Belorussia's important railway and industrial centers. Among other items, it manufactures prefabricated houses.

Belorussia's second largest city, Gomel (220,000), is situated in the southeastern corner of the country. It has been known since the twelfth century and is a busy river port. It is also an important railroad junction. The city's plants produce machine tools and farm and peat machines. The construction of a large superphosphate fertilizer plant is under way. Gomel also has wood-processing, leather-tanning, and food-processing concerns.

Brest has been in existence since 1017 and used to be an important fortress. Bypassed by the Germans in World War II, it long continued to defend itself against their rear. Remnants of its shattered fortifications—including the impressive fortress gate—still survive, reminding one of the grim story of those days.

7

★

THE SOUTHWEST:
THE UKRAINE AND MOLDAVIA

THE UKRAINE

 Geographically, the Ukrainian SSR is simply an extension of the Great Russian Plain, but in the north its difference from Belorussia is soon seen.

The Ukraine's wheat and corn fields, sugar beet farms, and orchards show an agricultural abundance. Except for the country's northern fringes, it is a mild and sunny land. At the subtropical maritime fringe of the Crimean Peninsula, the January average temperature is 39.2° F.

Ukrainian winters are interrupted by frequent thaws. Summer heat is followed by a long and delightfully sunny fall. During that equivalent of the Indian summer (which the Russians call "peasant women's summer"), Ukrainian woods of pine, beech, hornbeam, linden tree, and oak shine with the same magnificence of colors—green, bright red, brown, golden-yellow, orange—as one sees in New England.

A marked difference between the Great Russian and the Ukrainian villages leaps to one's eyes. Instead of the dark-gray, weatherbeaten Russian *izby* (log cabins), one sees in the Ukraine whitewashed *kháty,* cabins of boards daubed with clay and roofed with thatch or corrugated iron.

Unlike Russian villages, the Ukrainian ones are not arranged in a bare, monotonous line along a dirt road. In front of the *kháta* are cheerful sunflowers and hollyhocks, and behind are a kitchen garden, cherry and apple trees, and outbuildings. The farmsteads, most of them fenced, are crowded together. Often a pond with weeping willows is found beside the village.

In the Ukraine, as elsewhere in the Soviet Union, collective farmers are urged (and helped) to build more sophisticated houses, often for two or four families. With their appearance, village streets have begun to change, acquiring a suburban aspect.

Though larger than any European State outside of the European part of the RSFSR, the Ukraine is only 2.7 percent of the Soviet Union's territory. There are about 46 million inhabitants, or nearly 20 percent of the Soviet Union's population. Of these, 76 percent are Ukrainians—that is, the second largest branch of the Russian people and the second largest national component of the Soviet Union. Another 6 million Ukrainians or so live scattered in other Soviet republics.

The rest of the Ukraine's population is made up of Great Russians (18 percent of it), as well as of Jews, Belorussians, Poles, Moldavians, Bulgars, and Greeks. Except for the Russians, these smaller national groups live in the cities.

The role which the Ukraine played in Russia's early history is a great one. It was in Kiev, "the mother of Russian cities," that the first unified Russian State took shape in the ninth to twelfth centuries. At present, the Ukraine is particularly important in the national and in the economic life of the Soviet Union.

The republic is rich in natural resources and has, by Soviet standards, highly developed manufacturing industries. It accounts for nearly 50 percent of all pig iron produced by Soviet blast furnaces; 40 percent of steel; more than half of all iron ore and nearly one-third of all coal mined. It has very important manganese mines and substantial deposits of oil, natural gas, bauxites, antimony, mercury, and other minerals. The Ukraine is one of the Soviet Union's chief granaries. Over 20 percent of Russia's agricultural production, 57 percent of its corn, 42 percent of sunflowers, and 75 percent of sugar come from the Ukraine. About one-quarter of all Soviet cattle graze on Ukrainian meadows, and one-third of Soviet hogs are raised there.

These economic riches mean that the Ukraine is one of the most densely peopled regions of the Soviet Union. It has 182 inhabitants per square mile; half of them are city dwellers.

The Ukraine borders in the west on Poland, Czechoslovakia, Hungary, and Rumania; in the south on the Black and the Azov seas; in the north on Belorussia and on the Central Industrial and Black Earth regions; and in the east, on the Caucasus. It thus binds Europe to Asia and is European Russia's overland and warm-sea gateway to the West. More than half of the Soviet Union's maritime trade goes by way of Black and Azov seaports.

Who are the Ukrainians? What is the Ukraine?

By the middle of the fifteenth century most southwestern Russian principalities—including that of Kiev—found themselves, for reasons told elsewhere, under the Lithuanian and, after 1569, the Polish rule.

The Russians of that region remained Russians, and the peasants resented being serfs of Polish squires. Russians of all classes resented even more being virtually forced to become Roman Catholics. During the next two centuries, malcontents from these lands fled to a wide region along the middle Dnieper, known as the Dnieper *Ukraina,* or borderland.

In the Dnieper Ukraine there were some old (Kievan) cities and a growing number of new settlements. Officially, it was under Polish rule. But much of it was a "wild field," which neither Poland, nor Muscovy, nor the Crimean Tartars could control.

Here the fugitives became free Cossacks (the Tartar word for freebooters, or frontiersmen). Obeying no government save their own elective *hetman* (chief) and *krug* (circle), the Cossacks throve on hunting, fishing, some farming, and most of all by warring against their neighbors. to which their entire life was attuned.

Polish kings tried to use Cossack regiments as frontier guards but this did not work. Unruly Cossack bands attacked and sacked with especial gusto Polish nobles' opulent estates and entire Polish cities.

In 1648 the Cossacks, led by Bogdan Khmelnitsky, and joined by Russian peasants, successfully revolted against Poland-Lithuania. The western borderland, from the Donets River to the Carpathian Mountains, became independent. Eventually Khmelnitsky, regarded as the Ukraine's national hero, united it with Muscovy.

The Poles did not give up the Ukraine completely, however. For many years they battled with Muscovy for possession of the territory, and it was not until the end of the eighteenth century that most of the area was united.

After World War II the Soviet Union, or the Ukrainian SSR, finally received the last missing pieces of that territory—the Transcarpathian Ukraine (or Ruthenia), Galicia, and Northern Bukovina.

Between the twelfth and fifteenth centuries, the Russian dialects spoken in Southwestern Russia shaped themselves into what is known as the Ukrainian language. Though closely akin to the Russian, it is distinct from it and was probably influenced by the Polish tongue. The Ukraine, as a geographical term, gradually acquired the meaning of all territories inhabited by the Ukrainian-speaking people.

Dark eyes and hair are more apparent among the Ukrainians than among the "Great" Russians. There is much good-natured humor and, seemingly, a streak of laziness in them. They also are as indomitable a people as were their Cossack ancestors.

The Ukrainians hold in the Soviet life a place proportionately fully equal to that of "Great" Russians. They are well represented among Soviet Government ministers, diplomats, leading army commanders, scientists, managers of industrial plants, engineers, and writers.

At the base of the great Ukrainian plain lies a hard, continuous crystalline shield. It crosses the entire country, from Rovno in the northwest to the port of Zhdanov on the Azov Sea. Sedimentary layers

formed over the shield are cut in many places by canyonlike riverbeds and ravines. The Ukraine's main rivers are the Danube, the Dniester, the Western Bug, and the Dnieper.

In two regions, the Ukrainian plain is framed by mountains. Its protruding westernmost portion, bordering on Poland, Czechoslovakia, Hungary, and Rumania, is crossed by the Carpathian Mountains. The second mountainous region lies in the Crimea. It is formed by three parallel chains of Crimean Mountains running along the peninsula's southeastern shore.

Not all of the great Ukrainian plain is flat. Between the Dniester and the Southern Bug rivers, there is a wide range of hills up to 1,400 feet high, known as the Podolian Uplands. Farther east, between the Southern Bug and the Dnieper, the ridge is paralleled by similar Dnieper Uplands. The Azov Uplands parallel the Azov shore.

Within about 100 miles of the Black and the Azov seas, the uplands level out. The country becomes a flat plain. Round burial mounds of long extinct nomadic peoples are scattered on the plain here and there and they alone relieve the sunlit monotony of the sight. Such is, for instance, the landscape around Odessa or Nikolaev.

In the north, where the Ukraine borders on Belorussia, *Polesye*'s wooded and swampy lowlands overlap into the Ukraine for about sixty miles—and continue to bear that name. Then the swamps dry up and south of Kiev the forests thin out. The wooded steppe zone begins. At present, however, little of the original oak, maple, beech, linden and pine woods remain, except for patches along river valleys and ravines.

The wooded steppe and the northern half of the steppe zone form, together, a middle belt constituting three-quarters of the entire Ukraine. This belt crosses the country from west to east and runs from the Zhitomir-Kiev line in the north to Voznesensk and Nikopol in the south. Among the main provinces are those of Khmelnitsky, Vinnitsa, Cherkassy, Kirovgrad, Dniperopetrovsk, Poltava, Sumy, and Kharkov. Here, the soil is mostly *chernozyom*, or rich, fertile "black earth." The country, especially in its elevated areas, gets enough rain brought by western winds from the Atlantic.

This is a gently rolling land of endless wheat, corn or potato fields, and of beet, sunflower, and tobacco farms. The country is dotted with inviting Ukrainian villages, in some of which a church still stands. Here and there one sees a windmill; a caravan of trucks and ox-drawn carts carrying, on a dirt road, the crops to a collective farm's headquarters; a row of tall poplars standing guard around a former noble-man's manor house.

It is chiefly in this belt that the Ukraine's great agricultural wealth lies. Fifty-seven percent of the Soviet Union's corn and 42 percent of its sunflowers are produced here, as well as 75 percent of the Soviet Union's sugar, processed in Ukranian refineries.

The large acreage in sunflowers shows its importance to the Soviet economy. Its oil is used in the Soviet Union for food, in industry and (as oilcake) for fodder. Lightly roasted sunflower seeds are a delicacy to Ukrainian and Russian peasants. They sit after work in front of the *khata,* gossiping with neighbors and cracking and chewing the seeds.

The Ukraine may be divided into three large regions: the Donets-Dnieper Region, the Western Region, and the Southern Region.

The *Donets-Dnieper Region* includes nearly all of the "Left Bank Ukraine" and overlaps 200 miles to the west over the river's bend. In the south, it is confined by the Azov Sea; in the north lie its Chernigov, Sumy, Poltava, and Kharkov provinces.

During the last thirty years, oil has been discovered in several places. Near Poltava, the little neighboring city of Mirgorod and at Shebelinka near Kharkov natural gas has been found. Gas from Shebelinka deposits, which are very large, is now supplied by pipeline to Kharkov, Dniepropetrovsk, Kiev, Odessa, Moscow, and elsewhere.

In the Ukraine's narrow forest zone the ancient city of Chernigov has been known since the eighth century. Later it became the capital of a powerful principality, but its glory lies in the past. Now a small provincial city, it processes farm produce, engages in woodworking, produces synthetic fiber, and has a factory of musical instruments. Sumy, similar in size, is a sugar-refining center and produces fertilizers. The city of Poltava is somewhat larger and is crowded with gardens.

Poltava's name is, however, memorable for other reasons. In 1709, under Poltava's ramparts, Peter the Great inflicted a decisive defeat on Charles XII's seemingly invincible Swedish army which invaded Russia. In the world's eyes the Poltava Battle transformed Russia into a mighty power. The Podtava Province also gave Russia one of her greatest prose writers, Nikolai Gogol (1809–52).

An hour's train ride from Poltava is Kharkov, main city of the Donets-Dnieper Region, and the Ukraine's second largest city.

Founded in 1655 as a tiny Muscovite fortress on the northern fringe of the wild field, where Tartar raiders lurked, it was by the second half of the nineteenth century an important rail junction and a large machine-building and banking center. Today Kharkov has 1,090,000 inhabitants and hundreds of industrial plants. Perhaps the most important of these is its Tractor Plant, on which most of the Ukraine's collective farms depend.

The city is also a great cultural center and the headquarters in the Ukraine for the training of qualified engineering and technical personnel for industry.

Below Kharkov are found two of the Ukraine's greatest assets—the Donets Coal Basin and the Krivoi Rog iron ore deposits. It is the ideal combination of these sources of raw material for ferrous metallurgy that has transformed this section of the Ukraine into one of the most important industrial regions of the Soviet Union.

The Donets Coal Basin, or Donbas, sprawls on the Azov Uplands, along the Northern Donets. It is an area of some 10,000 square miles, about 170 miles long (east to west) and 35 to 60 miles wide, containing the largest amount (240 billion tons) of high-grade coal in European Russia.

Coal was discovered in the Donbas during the reign of Peter the Great. Mining there began at the end of the eighteenth century but it reached considerable proportions only a century later, when the first large steel foundries sprang up in the Dnieper Bend. Coal lies in the Donbas in thin seams alternating with flat sedimentary rock formations. Much of the land over the mines is cultivated; on the surface are wheat fields, peasant villages, and tractors at work, alternating with the hoisting towers over pitheads, huge mounds of excavated débris near the mines, and blast furnaces extracting metal out of iron ore near a railway station.

The main cities of the area are Donetsk (823,000) and Makeyevka (410,000) which have virtually fused into one city. This "double city" sits in the center of the coking coal district and produces about half of all metal smelted in the Donbas. Donetsk also has important plants building equipment for the mining industry, for steel mills, and for coke-chemical plants.

The city of Lugansk, founded in 1796 to cast guns and manufacture ammunition for the Russian Black Sea Navy, is now one of the main

Soviet manufacturers of locomotives. Among the Donbas's other industrial centers are Konstantinovka with important zinc and glass works and Gorlovka, which specializes chiefly in the production of nitrogen fertilizers and of coal-mining equipment.

The Krivoi Rog iron ore deposits lie about 180 miles east of the Donets Basin, along the Ingulets River, an affluent of the Dnieper. The city of Krivoi Rog, with half a million inhabitants, forms the heart of the mining area. Stretching for thirty-six miles along the Ingulets, it has absorbed into its site a number of mines and eleven railway stations serving them.

On the right bank of the Dnieper southeast of Krivoi Rog is the little city and river port of Nikopol. Nearby are located the largest deposits of maganese ore in the Soviet Union—and probably in the world. Small quantities of manganese are necessary for the production of especially tough kinds of steel.

In the Dnieper Bend, between Krivoi Rog and the Donbas, is an industrial area second in importance only to the coal country. Its main city—and river port—is Dniepropetrovsk (formerly Ekaterinoslav). Founded, in 1783, by Prince Potyomkin, Empress Catherine II's favorite statesman, it soon became an administrative, flour-milling, and commercial center, where landowners from the surrounding agricultural area came to sell their wheat, or to spend the winter.

In 1884, the Krivoi Rog-Donbas railway crossed it. Presently, iron works and machine-building plants cropped up in the city. Its population multiplied rapidly.

At present, Dniepropetrovsk has 790,000 inhabitants. New and greatly expanded old iron and steel works and machine-building plants are its main feature. It also has important coke-chemical, wood-processing, leather-tanning, shoe, and food-processing plants. Its geographical position, the five railways fanning out of it, and the Dnieper have made it the main transportation center in the area.

Zaporozhye, second largest city of the area, lies sixty miles south of Dniepropetrovsk and immediately south of the Dnieper Rapids. Founded in 1770 as Alexandrovskaya Fortress, it became the first river port below the Rapids to trade in grain. Its pre-Revolutionary farm-machinery plant supplied the entire surrounding agricultural area. But much of the present-day Zaporozhye, with its wide, tree-lined avenues and squares, is a new city.

Its chief industrial concern is the Dnieper Combinat, consisting of large metallurgical, high-grade steel, coke-chemical, and aluminum

works. Zaporozhye (including the Combinat), as well as Dniepropetrovsk, Krivoi Rog, and other neighboring areas get electricity from
the Dnieprogres, or the Dnieper Hydroelectric Power Plant named
after Lenin.

The Dnieper is being reconstructed along the same lines as the
Volga and some other rivers. The aim is to deepen it for navigation
and to make it generate cheap electric power. The huge concrete dam,
convex in shape, was completed in 1932, with the help of American
engineers and machinery, before Zaporozhye. The raising of the
Dnieper by it has obliterated—that is, flooded—the river's ten rapids
in the Bend. Formed by a crystalline ridge at the bottom of the river,
they obstructed shipping for over fifty miles. Navigation on the river
has been greatly improved by it.

The plan of the overall reconstruction of the Dnieper calls for the
erection of six sets of such dams, which will back the reservoirs
("seas"), power plants, and locks built into the river. Besides the
Dnieprogres, two of them are already in existence at Kremenchug
(110 miles above Zaporozhye) and at Kakhovka (about the same distance below it).

Three more sets of such dams and power plants along the Dnieper
are under construction. When completed, they will transform the river
into a chain of artificial reservoirs similar to those on the Volga.

The Dnieper is most important for industrial transportation but
passenger liners ply it, too. On the right bank are cliffs and clumps
of trees sloping down toward the river, villages, orchards, former
noblemen's manor houses with lofty columns; on the left bank fields
extend endlessly. Here and there the ship skirts an island. At the little
town of Kanev (known since the twelfth century), wide steps lead
uphill from the river to a large monument over the grave of Taras
Shevchenko. The Ukrainians regard the nineteenth-century Shevchenko as their greatest national poet. His statues and squares or
streets named after him are to be found in most Ukrainian cities.

Some sixty miles up the Dnieper, the panorama of a large city opens
up—Kiev. Its apartment houses, churches, gardens, factories, chim-
neys, parks, sloping down from the hills of the right banks, spill over
also on the flat left bank. On one of the highest hills, over a cliff, is
a large statue of a man in a long robe standing by a cross. This is
the statue of Grand Duke Vladimir who, in about 988, converted his
subjects to Christianity and whom the Russian Church reveres as a

saint. The ship crosses that very portion of the Dnieper into which, on that momentous day, the Russians dumped their heathen idols.

Belonging to the *Western Region,* Kiev is not only the Ukraine's capital, but, with its population of 1,383,000, the country's largest metropolis and perhaps the Soviet Union's loveliest city as well. Historically it was the cradle of both the Ukraine and Russia itself. Situated on hills and rich in greenery, it treats the visitor to one scenic effect after another. From the Vladimir Mountain a fascinating panorama opens up on the Dnieper with its bridges down below on the lower city and on endless fields and far-off woods on the opposite bank.

In the twelve hundred years of its history, Kiev has had periods of greatness and decline, of prosperity and misery. In the middle of the twelfth century it rivaled Constantinople in magnificence, according to Western witnesses. Soon afterward, it was sacked and reduced to charred ruins by the Tartars. From 1320 to 1654 it formed part first of Lithuania, then of Poland. Kiev lay once more in ruins in 1943, when the Nazis had been driven out of it. On its central boulevard, few of the remaining buildings were more than bombed-out shells.

But heavy wartime wounds have been healed and the city is now smarter than before the German invasion. The remarkable Cathedral of St. Sophia still rears its golden domes into the sky. Preserved inside are invaluable mosaics and frescoes dating from 1037.

Kiev's industrial role is important and diverse. Besides constructing machinery of various types, it also builds river ships and trolley cars, produces woolen and silk tissue and synthetic fiber, and has various food-processing plants.

Kiev is even more important as the seat of the government of one of the two principal SSR's and, above all, as a great cultural center, third after Moscow and Leningrad.

South, southeast, and southwest of Kiev there is a whole group of "sugar cities," such as Cherkassy, Vinnitsa, and Khmelnitsky. Scattered over a wide sugar beet country, they thrive chiefly by sugar processing.

West of Vinnitsa, across the upper Dniester, is the Carpathian area of the Western Ukraine. This is roughly formed by the Lvov-Ternopol-Chernovtsy-Uzhgorod line and lies in the Carpathian Mountains. In the northwest, beyond the Ukraine's borders, these mountains extend into Czechoslovakia and Poland, and in the southeast, far into

Rumania. That area's main sections are Galicia (with Lvov, Drogo-bych, Ternopol as its main centers), Bukovina (around Chernovtsy), and the Transcarpathian Ukraine (around Uzhgorod-Mukachevo-Khust).

The Carpathians are not very high. The loftiest summit of their Ukrainian section does not exceed 5,600 feet but their chains, over-grown with forests, dotted with mirrorlike lakes, cut by mountain streams, and topped by rugged rocky summits of different colors are wild and picturesque. The area attracts numerous Soviet vacationers.

This is the only region of the Ukraine still inhabited by the brown bear. Among its population are some 300,000 Gutsuls, Carpathian mountaineers. In their national dress they resemble the Tyrolese and in some of their customs and traditions they differ from other Ukrain-ians. Their Gutsul horse is famed for its endurance. Heavily loaded, it can make sixty miles a day over mountain passes.

The acreage sown here to grain crops is small. An important place is held by potatoes, sugar beets, sunflowers, tobacco, and fruit. In Northern Bukovina there are vineyards. Cattle and sheep breeding are predominant on the Carpathian slopes. Much of the country is wooded, and lumbering is also an important item.

The area's mineral resources are considerable. Except for the Car-pathian ranges themselves, it is a highly industrialized and densely peopled part of the Ukraine. In Galicia's Carpathian foothills, at Borislav, oil is mined. The nearby city of Drogobych is the refining center. Natural gas fields are situated in the same Drogobych area. Their gas is conveyed by two pipelines—north to Belorussia and the Baltic Republics, and east, to Kiev.

Potash is mined also near Borislav. Along the headwaters of the Western Bug, large coal deposits have recently been found. In the southeast there are ample supplies of phosphorites; in Transcarpathia manganese and brown coal; and common salt mines at Solotvina have been worked for centuries.

By far the most important city of the Carpathian area, and of Galicia in particular, is the splendid, medieval Lvov (500,000). It is surrounded by hills, the highest of which is topped by the picturesque ruins of its ancient kremlin.

Lvov has wide, well-planned boulevards and parks and narrow, cobbled, medieval streets. And it is rich in fifteenth- to eighteenth-century churches and houses, remarkable for their architecture.

Founded around 1250 by Prince Daniel of the westernmost Russian principality of Galich-Volhynia, Lvov was named after his son Lev (Leo). In 1349, it was conquered by Poland and remained under its rule for about four hundred years. Besides being a Russo-Ukrainian center, it became also a very important Polish city—truly a cradle of Poland's history.

After belonging to Austria and then again to Poland, Lvov was reunited with the rest of Ukrainian lands in the Soviet Union in 1939.

Economically, Lvov holds the whole westernmost part of the Ukraine together. It is a very powerful communication center. Eight railways connect the various regions of the Ukraine and farther points. Lvov also produces buses, mining and gas industry equipment, instruments and farm machinery.

The Transcarpathian Ukraine's main center is the ancient Uzhgorod, first mentioned in the ninth century. Sitting in a hilly country astride the snaking Uzh River, it is earmarked by an ancient kremlin and the atmosphere of time-honored rusticity. It specializes in woodworking, including plywood production and furniture-making, and in food industries.

The Transcarpathian Ukraine—formerly called Transcarpathian Russia, or Ruthenia—has always been inhabited by Russians. But it belonged to Hungary (later, Austria-Hungary) for about eight hundred years. The Carpatho-Russians (as they called themselves) continued, however, to speak their native tongue and regard themselves as Russians. After the dissolution of the Austro-Hungarian Empire in 1918, Transcarpathia was transferred to the newly created Czechoslovakia. Yet after World War II Czechoslovakia ceded Transcarpathia to the Ukrainian SSR, in accordance with the wishes of the latter's population.

After Lvov, the largest city of the westernmost part of the Ukraine is Chernovtsy, the main center of Northern Bukovina. The latter is a tiny Ukrainian country lying east of the Carpathians, along the Rumanian border. From the sixteenth century on it belonged to Turkey, Austria-Hungary, and Rumania, and was finally reunited with the Ukraine in 1945.

The Southern Region is composed of the provinces of Odessa, Nikolaev, and Kherson, which form, except for a rolling northern fringe, a belt of fifty to a hundred flat miles along the Black Sea shore; and the Crimean Peninsula, with mountains along only its southern edge.

Fields of wheat, corn, millet, and some pastures are predominant in the north. In the eastern part of the Kherson Province is Ascania Nova, a Soviet State reservation. Formerly it was a huge privately owned estate. In its zoological park, a great many Asiatic, American, and African wild animals, such as bison, ostriches, zebras, and others, live in natural conditions. Also, various experiments in hybridization and improvement of breeds of cattle are carried on here. Ascania also has areas of the original wormwood or feather-grass steppe found in the country before man put it under the plow.

Along the rivers and closer to the sea, fields give way to truck farms, melon fields, and orchards. Vineyards are numerous on sandy terraces descending to the limans—elongated, stagnant gulfs, formed when the sea flooded the lower part of riverbeds or valleys. Most of them are hemmed in from the seaside by sandbars. Villages in the region are quite large. Aligned mainly on river banks, some of them are several miles long.

The main city in this area is the gay, well planned Odessa (753,000). Sitting on a flat terrace shaped like a wide amphitheater, it overlooks a large, busy port. Its streets are lined with fragrant white acacia trees. Many of Odessa's buildings are made of a peculiar yellowish sandstone with small seashells embedded in it, which is quarried nearby. Around the city are numerous seaside and health resorts.

At the dawn of our era this was the site of Odessus, a Greek colony. In 1791 Russia won from Turkey the entire northern Black Sea shore east of the Dniester. Three years later Odessa was founded as a Russian naval base and commercial port.

The Russians put under the plow the virtually empty, fertile, brown-earth steppe. Novorossia (New Russia), as it was then called, developed rapidly. Odessa grew with it. The fact that Odessa's port never froze made it Russia's southern trade outlet into Western Europe. It acquired a special importance from the 1860's on, when railroads crossed the Ukraine to the seashore, and Russian wheat sailed via Odessa to Europe. The city lived in close contact with the Mediterranean world and borrowed its looks, cosmopolitan spirit, and exhilarating atmosphere. In Odessa's streets and cafes, Russians, Ukrainians, and Jews rubbed shoulders with a multitude of Greeks, Rumanians, Armenians, Italians, Frenchmen.

Now Odessa is one of the Soviet Union's main ports as well as a railroad terminal. It is also a great industrial center. From machine tools, pick-up trucks, and tractor plows to cinematographic equip-

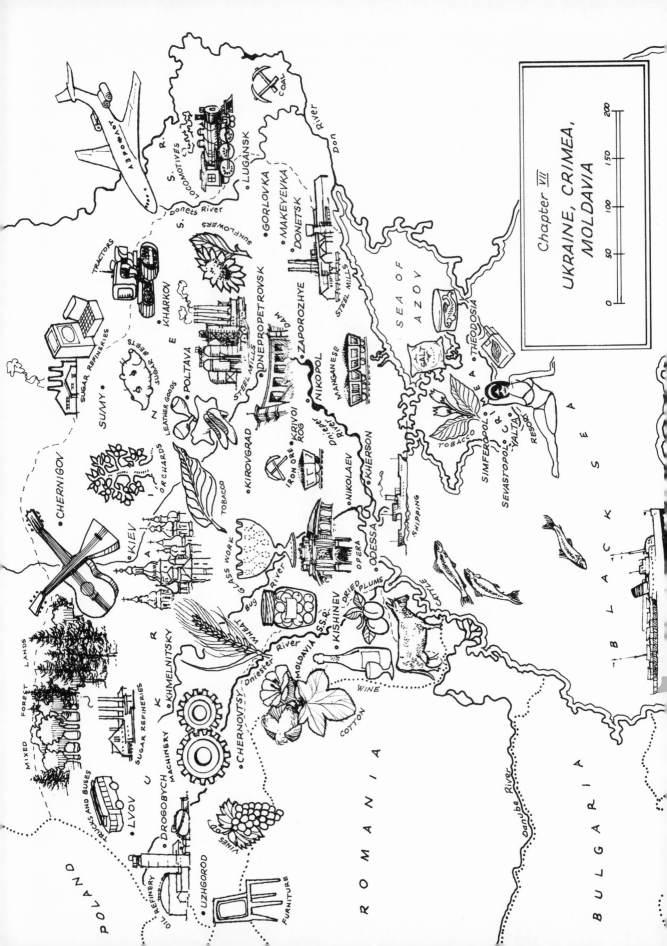

Chapter VII

UKRAINE, CRIMEA, MOLDAVIA

0   50   100   150   200

ment and fertilizers, it produces a variety of goods. With its twenty higher educational establishments, Odessa is one of the Ukraine's cultural capitals, and its university has produced a number of internationally known scientists.

Odessa has been declared a "hero-city" because of the desperately stubborn resistance which it put up during World War II when it was besieged and badly mutilated by enemy shells.

Other important cities of this part of the region are Nikolaev, sitting on the Southern Bug, and Kherson on the Dnieper's northern bank. Farther south the two rivers fuse together, forming one wide and long "Dnieper-Bug Liman," which opens up into the sea near the little historical fortress of Ochakov.

Nikolaev was founded as an eighteenth-century shipbuilding center and this still remains its main asset. One of the few Navigation Colleges in the Soviet Union is located there and it is a busy port as well.

Kherson—apart from shipbuilding, woodworking, and canning—is the "gateway port" for the entire Dnieper waterway. In particular, it is the chief distributor of Caucasian oil products over the entire Dnieper basin.

The westernmost Izmail District of the Odessa Province, between the lower Dniester and the Danube, borders on Rumania. Much of it —the so-called Budzhak Steppe—is good pasture land, but lacks water for farming. Wherever there is water, abundant orchards and vineyards are found. The little city of Izmail, once a Turkish fortress, on the Danube's northern branch, forming the Soviet-Rumanian frontier, is an important port for Soviet trade with the Danubean lands.

All along the Black Sea shore, there are fisheries and, in maritime cities, fish-processing and canning plants. The main commercial species caught are the herring, the mackerel, the gray mullet, sturgeon, and white sturgeon. Yet the Black Sea does not offer a great variety of commercial fish nor does the fishing industry play as great a role as along the Barents or White Sea shores.

The Black Sea has a strange peculiarity. Lower than a depth of about 650 feet, the water is contaminated with hydrogen sulphide which kills all living things except for some bacteria. Therefore, though the Black Sea is quite deep (up to 6,900 feet), there is no deep sea life in it.

The Crimea is joined to the mainland by the narrow Perekop Isthmus. The northern four-fifths of the peninsula are an extension of the flat, sun-scorched Kherson steppes, sown to wheat, corn, and tobacco. Its eastern shore, gleaming with white salt deposits, passes into an uninterrupted chain of stagnant, salt-water lagoons and swamps called *Sivash* (or Putrid Sea). The long Arbat sandbar isolates it from the Azov waters. In the Sivash, salt is extracted and there are large fisheries.

The northern Crimea suffers from drought even more than the Kherson area. Wherever there is water, wild hyacinths and peonies bloom in spring, and orchards and vineyards have been planted. Many of the Crimean rivers—including the largest, Salghir—dry up before reaching the sea. However, the situation is being remedied by a large irrigation project.

Farther south, the steppe begins to rise until, on a ninety-mile stretch between Sevastopol and Theodosia, it gives way to three parallel mountain ranges rich in marble, which run along the Black Sea. The combined width of all three ranges is about thirty miles. The highest and southern range, the Yaila, has elevations up to 5,060 feet. Its brownish-gray cliffs—crystalline in the west, limestone in the east —descend abruptly toward the sea, with isolated rocks rising out of the water. The shore between the Yaila and the beach is seldom more than three and a half miles wide.

The protection from northern winds offered by the Yaila makes the Crimea's narrow southern shore a "Soviet Florida," or "Mediterranean subtropics." A string of lovely seaside resorts is aligned here: Yalta, Miskhor, Alupka, Simeiz, Gurzuf, and Alushta. Surf bathing, hikes in the mountains, and beautiful scenery yearly attract hosts of vacationers. The shore is studded with hotels and rest homes, some of which were formerly palaces of wealthy individuals.

Colors are bright, the sea intensely blue, and the vegetation luxuriant along the shore. The change between fall and spring is hardly perceptible. Lombardy poplars, cypresses, eucalipti, Italian pines, olive and almond trees, and some of the palms are typical of the landscape; magnolias, oleanders, wistaria, and an endless variety of flowers are in bloom. There is a succession of parks, gardens, orchards, and vineyards climbing, together with villas, high up on mountain slopes. At a higher altitude are extensive tobacco plantations, for it is from the Crimea that the Soviet Union's best tobaccos come.

The Crimea (which the Greeks called Tauris) has had a dramatic history. Scythians, Goths, Huns, and Tartars swept into the peninsula by land. Greeks, Byzantines, and Italians came by sea.

In the fifteenth century the Crimea became a Tartar khanate, under the sovereignty of the Turkish sultans of Constantinople. For about three hundred years the Crimeans, often aided by Turks, raided and sacked Russian cities, abducted and sold Russians into slavery. In 1783 the Crimea was conquered and annexed to Russia.

Under the Soviets, in 1921, the Tartar Crimean Autonomous Republic was set up within the RSFSR. By 1939, there were about 250,000 Tartars in the Crimea; they formed a quarter of its population. During World War II the Crimea was occupied by Germans for three years, which had tragic consequences for its Tartars, accused by Stalin of cooperating with the Nazis. The Crimean Autonomous Republic was dissolved. Its territory was transferred to the Ukranian SSR as a mere administrative province, which it remains to this day. An overwhelming majority of Crimean Tartars were rounded up and summarily banished to Soviet Central Asiatic Republics.

It is onl in 1967 that the stigma of treason was removed from the Crimean Tartars. Yet they have not returned to their picturesque lands because other settlers, predominantly Ukrainians, are living there.

Now the Crimea's population consists of Russians and Ukrainians. Armenians, Greeks, Jews, and other national groups form but a small minority.

The Crimea's main city is Simferopol, full of gardens and on the banks of the Salghir in hilly country. It specializes in food processing (especially fruit canning), light industries, and machine-building. It is also the hub of a network of automobile roads, in which the Crimea is comparatively rich.

Sevastopol, about forty miles to the southeast, was founded in 1784 as a naval base. It commands one of the best harbors in the world. Sevastopol's epic defense in the Crimean War of 1854–55 won it world fame, and Tennyson made it the subject of his *The Charge of the Light Brigade*. Leo Tolstoy was among the defenders of the doomed fortress, and wrote about it afterward. Quite as remarkable was the defense Sevastopol put up during World War II.

Little Theodosia, besides being a busy port, engages chiefly in tobacco processing. But in the fifteenth to eighteenth centuries, when it was known as Kaffa, it was the main Crimean slave market for

Russians abducted during raids on Muscovy. Packed like cattle into ships' holds, they were shipped to Constantinople, Ismir, and Alexandria.

The Crimea's narrow eastern portion is known as the Kerch Peninsula. Kerch, its main city, sits in the northeastern corner, bordered by the Azov Sea and the narrow Kerch Straits which separate the Crimea from the Caucasus.

Near Kerch is one of the largest iron ore deposits in the Soviet Union. The Kerch Straits is rich in fish, and the city is the Crimea's main fishing, fish-processing, and canning center. Kerch herrings are well liked in the Soviet Union. Kerch is also a ferry station: Crimean railroad trains are ferried across the Straits from the city to the Caucasus.

A very old city, Kerch was first a Greek colony named Panticapaeum in the seventh century B.C. Then for centuries it was the capital of the prosperous Greek Kingdom of Bosporus. Numerous finds have been made there by Russian and Ukrainian archeologists, such as gold and silver vases with low reliefs and combs over 2,500 years old, and burial vaults of the first century of our era with remarkable mosaics.

MOLDAVIA

The Moldavian SSR, squeezed in between the Ukraine in the south, east, and north, and Rumania in the west, is one of the smallest of the fifteen Soviet Union republics. It is no larger than Massachusetts and Connecticut combined.

Moldavia's natural western border is formed by the Prut River, a tributary of the Danube. In the east its border parallels the Dniester, overlapping it in some areas. Nearly all of the Dniester (except for its northern section) and the lower course of the Prut are navigable. All of Moldavia is cut up by tributaries of these two rivers, flowing mainly in deep valleys and ravines.

The country's entire central part is occupied by the Kordy Elevation, which reaches a height of 1,200 feet. The rolling Beltsy Steppe slopes down to the north. South of the Kordy lies the Budzhak Steppe, a section of which continues on in the Odessa Province.

Though small, Moldavia has a population of 3,368,000, which makes it the most densely peopled of the union republics: it has nearly 230 inhabitants per square mile.

The Moldavians form 65 percent of the republic's population. They are closely related to Rumanians and, to some extent, to Ukrainians. Their language is a mixture of Rumanian (Romance) and Slavic (chiefly Russian and Ukrainian) words.

The remaining percentage of the republic's population consist of Ukrainians, who live in the north and along the Dniester; Bulgars in the south; Russians, Greeks, Armenians, and Jews in the cities.

Unlike the Ukraine, Moldavia does not hold any great mineral wealth. There are only building materials (limestone, sandstone, clays), phosphorites, some brown coal and, in the south, indications of oil and natural gas. Moldavia's wealth—and it is a wealthy land— is chiefly agricultural. It is an even sunnier and milder country than the regions of the Ukraine lying at the same latitude; a country of intensely black, fertile earth, orchards, and vineyards; of wheat and corn fields and of sunflower, sugar beets, and tobacco plantations.

This accounts both for the high density of Moldavia's population and for its distribution. Only 25 percent of the republic's population live in cities, which are few and mostly small. The country's only large city is its capital, Kishinev.

The great majority of Moldavia's population is rural. The villages of *kháty* similar to the Ukrainian ones are usually large, often numbering from one to three thousand people. In the valley of the Dniester some of them fuse together, forming entire chains of villages.

From the fifteenth to the nineteenth century, Moldavia was under the Turkish rule. The entire territory between the Dniester and the Prut was won by Russia through the War of 1806–12, and formed in Imperial Russia one administrative province, Bessarabia. During the hectic period of the Soviet Revolution, in 1918, Bessarabia was separated from Russia and became part of the ethnically kindred Rumania. Moldavian areas on the eastern bank of the Dniester alone remained part of the Soviet Union. They were formed into a small Moldavian Autonomous SSR.

In 1940 the Rumanian Government restored Bessarabia to the Soviet Union. The tiny Moldavian ASSR was joined with it to form the present-day Moldavian SSR.

Moldavia is becoming more and more of a wine- and fruit-producing country. These two branches of rural economy account, on the average, for 40 percent of the income of its collective farms and for about 75 percent of their income in the country's central region.

Kishinev is an attractive provincial city of 293,000 people. It is buried in gardens, and its streets are lined with white acacias, lindens, and poplars. Its chief industries are wine-making, canning, and tobacco processing.

8

★

THE CAUCASUS

Not quite as large as Colorado and New Mexico put together, the Caucasus is shaped like an immense isthmus between the Black and the Azov seas in the west and the Caspian Sea in the east. It joins Europe to Asia. For the Southern Caucasus, or Transcaucasia, borders on Asiatic countries—Turkey and Iran.

This is one of the most colorful regions of the Soviet Union, rich in striking contrasts. It offers almost every type of nature—endless fertile steppes, arid sand deserts, moist subtropical areas where palms, tea shrubs, oranges, and lemons grow, and nearby, the highest snow-capped mountains in Europe, from which mighty glaciers descend into valleys. Equally varied is the immense natural wealth concealed underneath that scenery. The Caucasus contains oil, natural gas, manganese, copper, lead, zinc, iron, tungsten, molybdenum, various rare metals, and coal. Caucasian rivers, lavishly fed by the glaciers of the Main Range, are an immense source of hydroelectric energy.

The Caucasus is earmarked by a remarkable ethnic variety. In its population of 24,847,000, the Russians and the Ukrainians together form a majority. However, forty languages are spoken in the Caucasus. Some of its peoples—like the Armenians and the Georgians in Transcaucasia—are comparatively large, and they belong among the oldest civilized peoples. Other groups—such as the Aguls, the Laks, the Chechens—are tiny nationalities. Unsurpassed horsemen, some of these mountaineers still wear their medieval costume and strictly observe ancient Muslim traditions. In far-off *auls* (Caucasian villages), the dagger at a man's belt is no ornament, and in that sunny land men are hot-blooded.

The Main Caucasian Range, crossing the entire country, divides it naturally into the Northern Caucasus and Transcaucasia. All of the Northern Caucasus, including the autonomous republics of its Mountainous Area is part of the RSFSR, but Transcaucasia comprises three union Soviet republics. They are the Georgian, the Armenian, and the Azerbaidzhanian SSR's.

THE NORTHERN CAUCASUS

The Northern Caucasus has a population of 13,450,000, of whom three-quarters are Russians and Ukrainians; they form an especially large majority in the Caucasian Foreland. The remaining quarter of the people belong to various native nationalities and live chiefly in the mountaineer republics.

The Foreland is well over half of the entire Caucasus, including the Rostov Province in the north and the Krasnodar and the Stavropol Territories south and southeast of it.

The Rostov Province is a direct extension of the Donbas, accounting for 12 percent of its coal production. Its main city, Rostov-on-the-Don, as well as smaller ones such as Taganrog and Novocherkassk, are industrial cities of the type found in the Donbas. Rostov, in particular, is a great builder of farm machinery; it also engages in ship repairing, food processing, and light industries. It is a busy sea and river port, whose importance has increased since the Volga-Don Canal, opened in 1952, has linked the two great rivers. The creation of the 216-mile-long Sea of Tsimlyansk on the Don, serving as a link in that canal system, has made the entire lower section of the river navigable for deep draught vessels. The area has also acquired a mighty hydro-electric power plant at Tsimlyansk which made possible an extensive irrigation system in the droughty eastern sections of the province.

Most of the Caucasian Foreland is a plain, gently sloping in the west toward the Azov and the Black Seas, and in the east to the Caspian Sea. In the middle of the plain lies the Stavropol Plateau, gradually rising in the south toward the Main Range.

That plateau stops the humid Mediterranean winds. Thus the western part of the plain gets adequate moisture. Fertile black earth steppe stretches to the horizon and the climate is mild.

This is one of the Soviet Union's most productive farming areas—the country of tractors, combines, and successful collective farms. Fields of wheat, corn, sunflower, and sugar beets alternate with soy beans and tobacco farms, orchards and melon fields. An increasingly important place is held by vineyards, especially along the seashore.

The southwestern part of the Krasnodar Territory overlaps the last offshoots of the Main Range and reaches the Black Sea shore. Its stretch from Tuapsé to Sochi, sheltered from the north, is subtropical in climate and vegetation, and has lovely scenery. The Russians rate its seaside resorts even higher than those of the Crimea.

There are extensive plowlands east of the Stavropol Plateau as well. The farther east, the more prone to drought is the country. In Daghestan (easternmost of North Caucasian republics), the annual precipitation is half that of the west. Stretches of wormwood or saline steppe, and of sand desert appear; occasionally a salt-water lake glitters in the sun. This is the Caspian Depression visited by arid winds from Central Asia's deserts. The percentage of land under plow declines rapidly and the area is used instead for sheep breeding, both for wool and for meat.

Except for the lower Don which only crosses the Rostov Province, all North Caucasian rivers are born from the glaciers of the Main Range and never lack water. The largest are the Kuban, cutting, with its many tributaries, across the Krasnodar plain to the Azov Sea; and the Kuma, the Terek, and the Sulak, flowing into the Caspian Sea. The abundance of water has aided irrigation and power plants. In marshy river estuaries—and on irrigated lands—rice is grown. The estuaries are also the home of stags, jackals, pheasants, and a variety of waterfowl.

There is a saying that the Main Caucasian Range has lavishly scattered great treasures at its feet. This is quite true if for "treasures" one substitutes "mineral resources."

The most important North Caucasian oil deposits all lie within short distances of the Range. The oldest of these fields—those of the Grozny-Malgobek area—have been worked since 1893. In some others, extraction has begun only recently. Pipelines join these fields together and to the main refining centers.

Very large natural gas deposits are located near Stavropol and

Krasnodar and they are piped to such faraway cities as Moscow and Leningrad. In the Soviet Union natural gas is playing an increasingly important role, not only as a fuel but also as raw material for nitrogen fertilizers and for various synthetic substances.

Lead is mined in the Elbrus deposits, copper at Urup, and coal nearby in the little Karachai-Circassian Autonomous District of the Stavropol Territory. Nearby, in the Kabardino-Balkar ASSR, there are important molybenum and tungsten mines. Still farther east, the Sadon area of the North-Osetian ASSR is rich in zinc, lead, and silver. There are various non-ferrous and rare metals in Daghestan.

The largest city of the Caucasian Foreland after Rostov is Krasnodar (395,000), formerly known as Ekaterinodar. It won universal notice during the revolutionary Civil Wars in Russia (1917–1920), when it was one of the headquarters of the White (anti-Soviet) Armies of South Russia.

Sitting on the right bank of the Kuban, which is wide and navigable here, Krasnodar is an important oil-refining center, produces machine tools and spare parts for farm machinery, and has a large worsted cloth combinat, a meat-packing plant, and a tobacco factory. It is also a rail junction. Incidentally, due to the Krasnodar Territory's wealth in farm produce, there are food-processing plants and canneries in most of the cities. Thirteen new sugar refineries have been set up in the last ten years, owing to a rapid expansion of growing sugar beets.

The Foreland's main Black Sea ports are Novorossiysk, Tuapsé, and Sochi. The first two, which are also oil-refining centers, ship oil and its products by tanker. Novorossiysk ships also large quantities of grain from the entire area. Sochi, itself a great seaside resort with modern American-type hotels, handles most of the maritime passenger traffic to the Caucasus.

Stavropol (171,000), administrative center of the Stavropol Territory, has various food industries and a fairly important machine-building plant.

In the southern part of the area are wooded mountains on a plateau; the highest of these is only 4,200 feet. At the foot of these mountains are numerous mineral springs, both hot and cold. Russian physicians value them greatly for medicinal purposes. Watering resorts sprang up there in the nineteenth century—of which Kislovodsk and Pyatigorsk are the most important.

The 10,080,000 Russians and Ukrainians of the Northern Caucasus live chiefly in the Foreland. The Ukrainians form a great majority in the west, especially along the Kuban and its affluents, and the Russians are found in the east.

The 3,370,000 Caucasians of non-Russian nationalities inhabit the Mountainous Area which forms the southern fringe of the Northern Caucasus, narrow in the west, but widening considerably in the east. Some of these little peoples came to the Caucasus centuries ago. Others have always lived there.

They fall into three main linguistic groups: the Turkic group, represented by the Nogai Tartars, the Kumyks, the Karachais, and others; the Iranian group, to which belong the Osetians and the Tats; and the Caucasian group proper, the Circassians, the Kabardinians, and the Chechens.

The Russians came into contact with the Caucasian wild field in the sixteenth century; its real colonization began two hundred years later. At first this was carried on chiefly by Cossacks. Those who settled along the lower Kuban were Ukranian Cossacks. Farther east, penetrated the Don Cossacks, who had formerly fought the Crimean Tartars in South Russian steppes.

Mohammedan mountaineers—especially the Lezghins, the Chechens, the Kabardinians, the Circassians—raided the Cossacks, who reciprocated in kind. Then the Russian Government assumed an active role. In 1765 it built a fortress in the very heart of the Caucasus, and began to set up a "fortified line" from Azov to the Caspian Sea.

In 1834 a fanatical and remarkable leader, Sheikh Shamil, appeared among the mountaineers. With Turkey's help he raised the banner of a Moslem Holy War against the Russians and inflamed many of his followers with great enthusiasm. War went on for twenty-five years until finally mountaineer *auls* began to defect to the Russian side. As a result, Shamil's main forces were crushed and he was taken prisoner.

The defeated mountaineers (and especially Shamil himself) were treated with great deference by the Tsars' Government. Those who wished to do so were allowed to emigrate to the Moslem Turkey. Mountaineer chieftains received the status of Russian noblemen and peace was soon achieved in the Caucasus.

When the Soviets came to power they met with a determined resistance from both the Russian and the mountaineer population of the Caucasus. Even after the Communist victory some of the mountaineer peoples continued to carry on guerrilla warfare against the Soviets.

Native peoples of the Northern Caucasus form compact ethnic groups in their respective enclaves of the Mountainous Area. These enclaves have been divided under the Soviet regime into two autonomous districts (or AO's) and four autonomous Soviet Socialist Republics. Such districts have a lesser degree of self-government than autonomous republics, but are equal to them in cultural autonomy.

The Mountainous Area is a peculiar world. Usually the *auls* are small. In some—especially on the plain—there are dwellings resembling the Ukrainian *kháty*, and a growing number of modern collective farmers' cottages. Predominant are the traditional *sákli*, built of fieldstone, flat-roofed, and leaning against a vertically cut slope of a rock which serves as its back wall. A poor *sáklia* may be furnished with little more than a rug. The *sákli* usually cluster together for safety. In some *auls*, groups of related families still have a square battle tower of their own, where in the past they could withstand a siege. Even now blood feuds, passing from generation to generation, still exist in far-off *auls*.

Most of the mountaineers have regular, well-chiseled features and athletic bodies, though they are not necessarily tall. Many are still Mohammedans.

The tiny Adyguey Autonomous District (AD) has a population of 360,000, of whom about half are Adygueys, and lies along a tributary of the Kuban. Wheat, tobacco, and sunflowers are the main crops,

along with orchards; there is sheep and horse breeding. The district's capital is Maikop, center of the Maikop oil region.

The next five are all adjacent to one another. Their southern borders lie high up in the mountains of the Main Range and they descend to the north, down the heavily wooded slopes to the treeless plain.

The economy and way of life in all these little national enclaves are similar: farming on the plain with orchards and vineyards; work in mines or oil fields in the foothills; sawmilling on the mountain slopes; and animal husbandry (sheep, horned cattle) higher up on the Alpine meadows.

The Karachi-Circassian AD, first of the five, lies below the two-headed snow-capped Mount Elbrus (18,468 feet). This is the highest peak in the Main Caucasian Range—and in all Europe. The territory is crossed by the Kuban River which has originated out of one of Elbrus's glaciers and is here a whirling, roaring mountain stream. The district has 327,000 inhabitants and the capital is Cherkessk. The mountainers work in the coal, the Elbrus lead, and the Urup copper mines.

Then comes the Kabardinian-Balkar ASSR, with a population of 520,000. The Kabardinians inhabit the fertile plain. The Balkars, second of the republic's two peoples, live in the mountains and engage in lumbering and animal husbandry. Tungsten and molybdenum mines are also important. In Nalchik (114,000), the capital, there are a metallurgical plant, a furniture factory, a meat-packing combinat, and other food-processing concerns. Nalchik is also a starting point of expeditions into the snow-capped part of the Range. A large hydro-electric power plant has brought electricity to the vicinity of glaciers and to a wide area on the plain.

The Adygueys, the Circassians, and the Kabardinians, inhabiting these three national units, are different branches of the same Circassian people (of the Caucasian group). There are now altogether about 360,000 of them. The Karachais and the Balkars, on the other hand, are Turkic nationalities.

Progressing eastward, the North Osetian ASSR is next. Unlike most other North Caucasian mountaineers, the Osetians, forming a half of the republic's population of 510,000, are an Iranian-speaking people —descendants of the medieval Alans (or Alani). They were Christians since early times and have kept their faith although in the seventeenth century Mohammedan (Kabardinian) princelings subjugated them.

The capital is Ordzhonikidze, formerly Vladikavkaz. Founded in 1784 as a Russian fortress in a wild, unfriendly land, it is an industrial city, especially well known for its non-ferrous metallurgy plant.

Still farther east lies the Chechen-Ingush ASSR, with a population of 1,008,000. The Northern Caucasus's important Grozny-Malgobek oil fields are located here. Grozny, seat of the republic's government, and also a former Russian fortress dating back to 1819, is now a large industrial center.

During World War II, as the Germans fought their way into the Northern Caucasus, the Chechens and Ingushes took that opportunity to rise against the Soviets again. Along with other mountaineers who had joined them, they were banished to Kazakhstan and Western Siberia, and their autonomous lands dissolved. Some of these people perished of hunger, cold, or inability to adapt themselves to the rude change. In 1957 they were finally brought back to their *auls*, and the autonomy of their lands was reestablished.

The easternmost territory in this group of five is the Daghestan ASSR. Bordering on the Caspian Sea it is comparatively large, with a population of 1,325,000. These people belong to over thirty nationalities, speaking as many languages and dialects. Among them are the aboriginal Caucasian Avarians, Lezghins, and Darghins; the Turkic-speaking Kumyks and Nogai Tartars (the latter's ancestors were among Muscovy's Tartar rulers).

In early times some of these peoples retreated to little accessible mountain valleys, fleeing from wars and other dangers that threatened them on the plain. These valleys, less arid than the lowlands, are better suited for agriculture, although both areas are put to use. Daghestan is a great sheep and cattle country—in the summer animals graze on mountain pastures. In winter collective farmers drive them down to the Caspian steppes.

Like other Caucasian mountaineers, Daghestanians have inherited from the Middle Ages various handicraft industries, from carpet-weaving to ceramics and goldsmithery. Silver and golden objects of Caucasian workmanship have their own distinctive style.

Daghestan's capital is Makhachkala. Until recently it was known as Petrovsk, for it had grown out of a fortress founded by Peter the Great. It is a very important rail, shipping, and fishing center. Oil is extracted offshore from the city and farther south new natural gas deposits are being developed.

Makhachkala contains a branch of the Academy of Sciences of the USSR. With the help of the Academy the written language of many North-Caucasian nationalities save been worked out.

The Main Range, with two side ranges paralleling it in the middle, crosses the Caucasus diagonally. In the northwest, hills begin near the little Taman Peninsula, jutting, between the Black and the Azov seas, toward the Crimea. Over 680 miles to the southeast it flattens out in the Apsheron Peninsula, which protrudes into the Caspian Sea.

The western third of the Main Range does not rise above 10,500 feet. The central and highest part is an almost uninterrupted line of lofty peaks, capped with eternal snow and ice. Ten of these peaks— among them Mount Elbrus—are higher than Mont Blanc (15,771) in the Swiss Alps. Some of them are extinct volcanos. Farther east, though still counting impressive summits, the range gradually tapers down and finally breaks up into intricate chains of hills.

The slopes of all the ranges are heavily wooded up to the altitude of 7,800 feet. The beech, alder, hornbeam, oak, maple, linden, and poplar are found in the lower belt. Higher up is the coniferous forest of fir, silver fir, and pine. These forests are alive with deer, bears, wolves, foxes, lynxes, some leopards and jackals.

Higher up, the woods give place to sub-Alpine, bright-green meadows with flocks of sheep, alternating with fields of red and white rhododendrons and—still higher—yellow primroses. The grass vanishes; the first patches of snow appear and stay in the wrinkles of the terrain all summer. Mountain goats and eagles are the only visitors here. For still higher are nothing but tortured, twisted masses of ice of the descending glaciers, blindingly white snowfields, and sheer, dark, reddish-gray rocks.

TRANSCAUCASIA

Transcaucasia's territory is just over half that of the Northern Caucasus and its population is 11,402,000. Of the three union republics belonging to it, the Georgian SSR occupies the northwest, including the entire Transcaucasian portion of the Black Sea shore; the Azerbaidzhanian SSR lies in the east, including the Caspian shore; and the Armenian SSR is in the southwest. Along the Soviet Union's southern frontier Georgia borders on Turkey; Armenia on Turkey and Iran; and Azerbaidzhan on Iran.

Transcaucasia contributes a great deal to the Soviet economy. Oil and gas fields in Azerbaidzhan, manganese mines in Georgia, and the copper mines of Armenia are very important. The agriculture, subtropical in many areas, produces items which few of the Soviet Union's other regions can duplicate. Thus, on Georgia's warm, humid Black Sea shore, there are extensive citrus fruit and some fig tree and pomegranate plantations, and tea is grown in large quantities. By 1970

Georgia's tea crops should satisfy the needs of the entire Soviet Union. Transcaucasia is, furthermore, a country of wines and silk.

Aside from the economic aspect this area is rich in resorts spreading all along the Black Sea shore. A warm sea, mountain panoramas, magnificent vegetation, and healthful mineral springs combine here.

Transcaucasia was known to the peoples of antiquity. According to a Greek legend, it was here in the Caucasian Mountains that Prometheus was chained to a rock for having stolen fire from the gods and given it to men. And it was here, in the Colchis Plain, that the legendary Argonauts searched for the Golden Fleece.

Transcaucasia is far more mountainous than the Northern Caucasus. Over half of its territory lies more than 1,640 feet above sea level.

In the north the slopes of the Main Range continue, overgrown with dense woods. In Transcaucasia's extreme south is the huge Armenian Plateau, averaging an altitude of 4,950 feet, cut into canyons by streams and occupying about one-quarter of Transcaucasia. In the middle of that plateau is the large Lake Sevan.

The middle of Transcaucasia is a plain. It is cut by the transverse Surami Chain which forms a watershed. Along the Rion River in the west the plain slopes and expands toward the Black Sea, forming the fertile Rion Lowlands, known since antiquity as Colchis. In the east the plain follows the course of the Kurá River, greatly widens toward the Caspian Sea and forms lowlands, part of which lie below ocean level.

The picture is complicated by a number of minor ranges, which touch or cross the Armenian Plateau—such as the Adzhar, the Zanghezur and the Talyah mountains, referred to collectively as the Lesser Caucasus. None attain the altitude of the Main Range. The loftiest of their peaks is the cone-shaped, volcanic Mount Aragats, 13,440 feet high.

Transcaucasia belongs to the subtropical zone, but even though the Main Range shuts off cold northern winds the transverse ranges cause various climatic contrasts. As a rule, however, the country's west, reached by Atlantic winds, is moist; the east, exposed to the arid breath of Transcaucasian deserts, is dry.

The land is rich in vegetation and animals of all types. The animals of the Main Range are found in Transcaucasia as well, but animals of southern lands, such as the Indian porcupine and the antelope, are also encountered here.

THE GEORGIAN SSR

Out of the 4,548,000 inhabitants of the Georgian SSR, 64 percent are Georgians, subdivided into several branches, such as Kakhetians, Imeretians, and Svanetians. The rest of the republic's population includes Russians, Armenians, Azerbaidzhanians, and other minority nationalities. Three of them form autonomous units within Georgia—the South-Osetian AD and the Abkhazian and the Adzhar ASSR's.

The Georgians are a Hittite-Iberian race, one of the oldest civilized races. The Kingdoms of Colchis and of Iberia were known there in the sixth century B.C. and the Georgians embraced Christianity around A.D. 337. Ruins of fifth- and sixth-century churches still stand in various parts of the country. Long dominated by Persia and later by the Arabs, Georgia won back her independence in the eighth century. Her national culture bloomed in the reign of Queen Tamara (1183–1213).

After the sixteenth century, hammered by new invasions, the Georgians began to seek the aid of the Muscovite tsars. In 1801 the little country was annexed to Russia.

Tbilisi (830,000), Georgia's capital and Transcaucasia's second largest city, stands on hilly terrain and straddles the Kura River. It is a lovely city with tiled roofs, balconies over the river, and terraced gardens. In some sections are narrow and shabby Turkish-type streets; Tbilisi is a city of spirited, vivacious crowds. In it, Georgia's Mediterranean atmosphere is keenly felt.

The city was founded in the fifth century on a site containing hot springs (in Georgian *tbili* means hot). It is rich in relics of the past, such as the Zion Temple dating back to the sixth century and Metekh Castle with a thirteenth-century church, both of which have sharp, cone-shaped domes.

Tbilisi is an important center of light industries, processing chiefly Transcaucasian raw materials such as wheat, tea, grapes, wool, and silk. This is Georgia's cultural capital. Georgia has an old literature and a large and refined intellectual class.

Twenty miles southeast of Tbilisi, on the same main Transcaucasian Railroad linking the Black to the Caspian Sea, a large iron and steel mill and a chemical plant were founded in 1948. Since then, a whole new city has grown up around them—Rustavi.

West of Tbilisi is the tiny city of Gori, the birthplace of Joseph

Stalin. The Soviet Union's ruthless Communist dictator was a Georgian cobbler's son.

Farther west, a short side line branches off northward from the main railroad to the famed Chiatura manganese mines. These deposits are not Georgia's only mineral asset; coal is mined in the western part of the country and oil is extracted in the east, in the Shirak Steppe, which also contains natural gas and various ores.

The picturesque city of Kutaisi also borders the Transcaucasian Railroad line. Bright with gardens, it is Georgia's second largest city and the main industrial and rail center of the Colchis Plain. Known since ancient times, it now has an automobile assembly plant, plus silk, leather, and meat-packing combinats.

In Georgia, as in the Northern Caucasus, the steepness of mountain rivers gives the country a very high hydroelectric potential. A whole "cascade" of hydroelectric power plants has been built on the Rion and Kura rivers and their affluents, especially around Tbilisi and north of Kutaisi.

In most of Georgia's warm valleys, and especially in the fertile Rion Lowlands, much wheat and corn is grown. Orchards are plentiful, but truly typical of the land are the endless vineyards on the sunlit mountainsides. Wine-making is one of Georgia's national industries.

Georgia has three autonomous units.

The *South-Osetian AD* lies north of Gori, ascending high into the mountains, to the very crest of the Main Range. Beyond the crest, in the Northern Caucasus, lies the North-Osetian ASSR. The little group of Osetian people has been divided—both by physical geography and by the USSR's political structure—into two separate but neighboring parts.

As in the north, the Osetians here are Christians. They are predominantly sheep breeders and farmers. In the last decades they have become literate, and food-processing and woodworking concerns have appeared in the district. A spur of the Transcaucasian Railroad has been run to the district's border. Its main city, Tskhinvali—virtually a large *aul*—has 30,000 inhabitants.

The *Abkhazian ASSR* occupies Georgia's narrow northwestern strip. It has a population of 462,000, of whom 16 percent are Abkhazians. Christians since the 550's, the Abkhazians were conquered in the

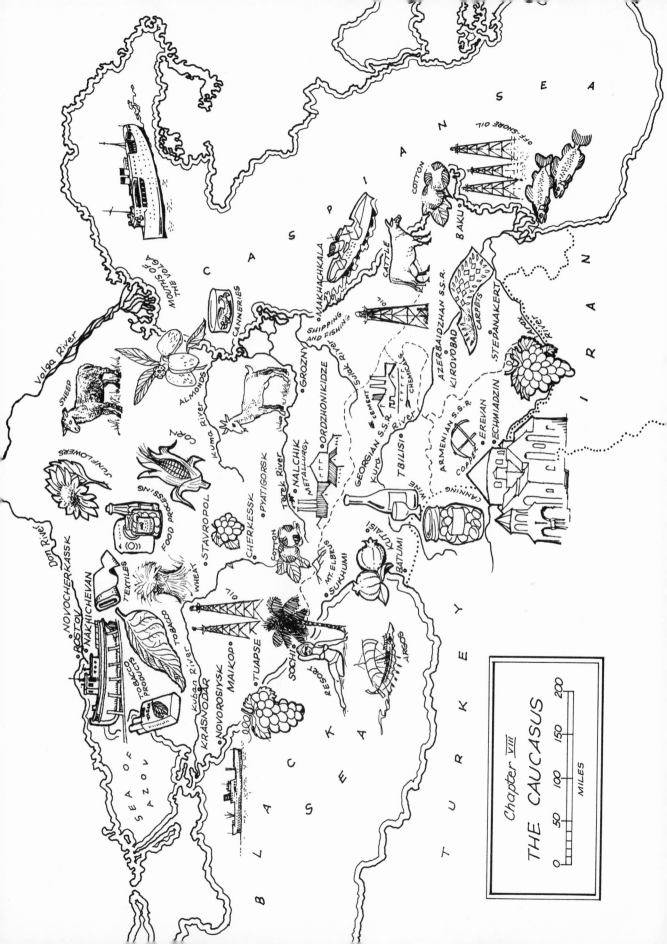

Chapter VIII

THE CAUCASUS

MILES
0 50 100 150 200

fifteenth century by the Turks and converted by them to Moham-medanism.

In the maritime strip of the ASSR, there are large tea, citrus fruit, tobacco, fig tree, and eucalyptus plantations. In the few cities are important tea, tobacco, and canning factories; also some leather-and-shoe and woodworking concerns. Sukhumi, the republic's capital, is situated at the head of a deep bay and is an important seaside resort. It is a picturesque city, whose sunlit streets are lined with palms, cypresses, and gardens.

The *Adzhar ASSR* occupies the southwestern corner of Georgia's Black Sea shore and has a population of 294,000. The Adzharians are Georgians whose ancestors were forced to embrace Mohammedanism at the time when their land was dominated by the Turks.

The land's capital and largest city is the port of Batumi, internationally known as the terminal of the oil pipeline leading across all Transcaucasia. Built in 1901, it was one of the earliest such pipelines in the world.

Batumi has a large oil refinery and is an important exporter of oil, tea, and canned foods. The city is attractive, rich in vegetation and —by Soviet standards—very up-to-date.

THE AZERBAIDZHANIAN SSR

Azerbaidzhan's territory is larger than Georgia by 20 percent. Out of its population of 4,660,000, 67 percent are Azerbaidzhanians and the rest Russians, Georgians, Armenians, and Kurds. It is—at least historically—a Moslem country.

The Azerbaidzhanians are a Turkic people. In the fifteenth to seventeenth centuries, the native Azerbaidzhanian State became a bone of contention between Persia, Turkey, and, later, Russia. The annexation of its northern half by Russia was completed in 1828. Azerbaidzhan's southern half continues to form part of Iran.

Azerbaidzhan is not as mellow and inviting a land as Georgia. The rainfall is only one-third that of Georgia. Lowlands occupy 40 percent of its territory, and mountains over 4,500 feet high only 12 percent. Some areas of the country lie below ocean level and are virtual deserts.

Agriculturally, therefore, Azerbaidzhan is not nearly as rich as Georgia. Up to 70 percent of the crops exist by artificial irrigation, which the Soviet authorities have been energetically developing. Especially important is the fifty-mile-long Minguechaur Reservoir constructed on the upper Kura, which feeds a network of canals southeast in the thirsty Kura Lowlands.

However, Azerbaidzhan is not a poor country. The sources of its wealth are fish, sheep, oil, gas, cotton, silk, and wool.

With a population of 1,175,000, Baku, dating back to the ninth century, is not only Azerbaidzhan's capital, but also the fourth largest city in the Soviet Union. It is a great industrial center, descending in an immense amphitheater to a horseshoe-shaped bay with the largest port on the Caspian Sea. A multitude of oil derricks rises here out of the sea, for it used to be the foremost oil producer in the world. Nearby, the "Oil Stones"—a whole town of housing blocks and industrial buildings—sits on steel piles in the open sea.

Kirovobad in the west of the republic is primarily a large textile center, but it also has a large aluminum plant. Ancient domestic crafts of silk and wool processing and of carpet-making flourish around the city, which traces its history back to the fifth century. It preserves some ancient, architecturally remarkable mosques.

In Azerbaidzhan's southwest, on a mountainous plateau with peaks up to 10,000 feet high, lies the *Nagorno-Karabakh AD*. Its population of 146,000 is predominantly Armenian, for across a river valley lies the Armenian SSR. However, the district's inhabitants have closer economic ties and better communications with Azerbaidzhan than with their Armenian brothers.

The Karabakhians engage chiefly in sheep, horned cattle and horse breeding. At adequate altitudes they also grow wheat, fruit, grapes, and mulberry trees (for the silkworm). Modern concerns— a silk combinat, wine and brandy distilleries, a knitting factory—have been built in the district. Stepanakert, its capital, has 27,000 inhabitants.

Finally, the *Nakhichevan ASSR*, also forming part of Azerbaidzhan, is separated from most of the country by a wide belt of Armenia. Its position is just the reverse of the Nagorno-Karabakh AD, for 85 percent of its population are Azerbaidzhanians, separated from their countrymen.

The republic which once upon a time was an independent Khanate of Nakhichevan, occupies the southern part of the Armenian Plateau. Seventy percent of the cultivated lands are artificially irrigated. Major crops are cotton and tobacco; some grain crops are grown; there are orchards and vineyards. Animal husbandry, of course, holds an important place. Nakhichevan, an ancient city with a population of 28,000, is the republic's capital.

THE ARMENIAN SSR

Less than half the size of Georgia, Armenia is the smallest of the fifteen union republics of the USSR. In the south, it borders on Turkey and Iran. It is a land-bound country, separated by some 100 miles from both the Black and the Caspian seas. Ninety percent of its territory lies more than 3,300 feet above ocean level. Armenia's population of 2,194,000 is comparatively homogeneous: Armenians form 88 percent and the remainder are chiefly Russians, Azerbaidzhanians, and Kurds.

In the ninth century B.C. there was a kingdom around Lake Sevan, the Urartu, whose inhabitants were direct ancestors of the Armenians. At that time and for centuries afterward, their territory reached out south and southwest into Asia Minor.

However, the Armenians' history was marred by tragedy. Their kingdoms were wiped out and towns turned to charred ruins by Assyrian, Arab, Tartar-Mongolian, Persian, and Turkish invasions. Massacres of Armenians by Turks and Kurds were a recurrent feature even of nineteenth-century history. Finally, after the Russo-Turkish war of 1878, the Armenians began to live in peace in the part of their national territory which had passed to Russia.

Armenians began to embrace Christianity in the fourth century, and a century later had a written language of their own. In the Middle Ages, their literature flourished. Armenian ninth- and tenth-century miniatures are internationally known and valued.

The Armenian landscape is one of scorching sun, dry air, cloudless sky, and bare, rocky mountain ranges framing burnt-out plateaus and hollows. Ruins of ancient stone fortifications or monasteries of the peculiar Armenian architecture, adorn some of the mountain slopes. Woods cover only 10 percent of Armenia's territory—chiefly north of Lake Sevan. Winters are colder here than in most other inhabited areas of Transcaucasia, with the January average, in some places, as low as −0.4° F.

Armenia's main river is the Arax, a tributary of the Kura. Most of its course serves as the USSR's frontier with Turkey and Iran. A tributary of the Arax, flowing out of Lake Sevan, plays an important role. Five large hydroelectric power plants built on it supply electricity to the country which lacks other sources of energy, such as coal or oil.

The country's main mineral wealth are copper ore deposits, plus iron ore and nepheline (raw material for aluminum). It is also very rich in building materials, from marble and tufa to fireproof clays.

Agriculture—chiefly on irrigated lands—is limited in acreage, but offers a considerable variety of crops. Sugar beets, cotton, tobacco, and sunflower as well as almond, fig, olive, and mulberry trees are among them. There are orchards, truck gardens, and vineyards. Cattle and sheep breeding are common and Armenia is known for its cheeses.

Erivan (652,000), the republic's capital, is one of its oldest cities. In the eighth century B.C. it was an Urartu fortress. Now its central part has wide asphalt boulevards lined with trees; the buildings of pink-violet tufa are adorned with intricate patterns. There is a beautiful view of the biblical Mt. Ararat, lying on Turkish territory across the border.

Erivan is also Armenia's main industrial city, producing electrical equipment, synthetic rubber, and artificial fertilizers. It also has canning, wine, and brandy-distilling and other food-processing concerns, as well as factories for various household items.

Tiny Echmiadzin is a museum-city. Built in the fourth century and surrounded by remarkable ancient buildings, it seems to live in Transcaucasia's Middle Ages. Its State Museum of Antiquities holds many a historical treasure—including over eight thousand ancient Armenian manuscripts. Echmiadzin is the seat of the Catalicos, or head of the Church of Armenia.

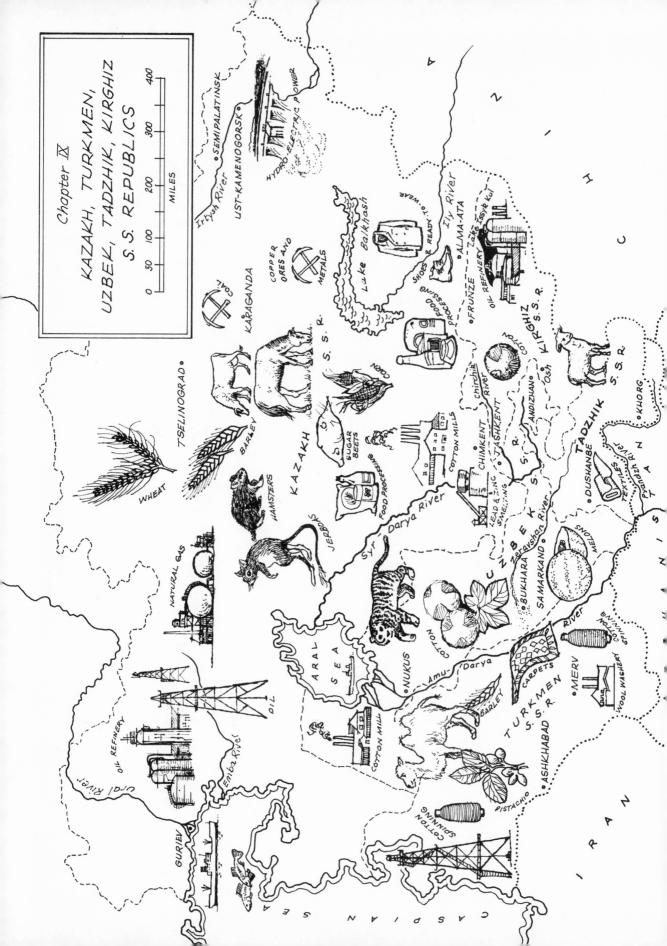

Chapter IX

KAZAKH, TURKMEN,
UZBEK, TADZHIK, KIRGHIZ
S.S. REPUBLICS

MILES

0 50 100 200 300 400

9

★

CENTRAL ASIA

 Soviet Central Asia is a huge country, about half the size of the United States, but with a population of only 29,890,000. It is 1,800 miles from the shore of the Caspian Sea and the lower Volga Region in the west to Sinkiang, a province of Chian, in the east; and 1,000 miles from the Urals and Western Siberia in the north to Iran and Afghanistan in the south.

Most of Central Asia is an immense plain. Well over half the country is sun-scorched semi-desert, made of clay, sand, or rock. At its southern and eastern edges, the plain rises, framed by some of the world's highest mountain ranges and plateaus.

The area holds great natural resources from oil, gas, coal, iron ore, manganese, and molybdenum, to nickel, copper, polymetallic ores (lead, zinc, silver), gold, asbestos, and phosphorite. It is only now that the exploitation of these riches—begun in the 1880's—has gotten under way in earnest. Besides, Central Asia is a very important sheep and cattle land. Among the deserts there are important farming regions which yield large crops of wheat, millet, fruit, vegetables, melons, and grapes, as well as 90 percent of the Soviet Union's cotton.

Central Asia has five union republics. Its northern two-thirds form the territory of the largest of them—Kazakhstan, or the Kazakh SSR —with a population of 12,130,000. Central Asia's southern third, formerly known as Turkestan, is divided into four union republics, the

Turkmen, Uzbek, Tadzhik, and Kirkhiz SSR's. Their total population is 17,267,000.

Since long before the beginning of our era, waves of invaders crossed Central Asia on their way west. Some settled there and intermixed, both with its earlier dwellers and among themselves. Of the country's present native peoples, the Kazakhs, Turkmen, Uzbeks, and Kirghiz belong to the Turkic group. The Kazakhs and the Kirghiz, however, have a strong Mongoloid strain, revealed by their broad, flattish faces. The Tadzhiks are Iranians with an Uzbek mixture, and they speak an Iranian tongue.

The country's native inhabitants have been devout Mohammedans for centuries, and many still are. Central Asia is the heart of the ancient Mohammedan world.

The entire western half of Central Asia is occupied by the Turanian Lowlands, with the Aral Sea lying northwest of its center. Not all of it is absolutely flat, for in the southwest, along the Iranian border, is the Kopet Dag Range, rising abruptly over the Turkmen SSR's sand desert. In the north, on Kazakhstan's territory, a spur of the Ural Mountains—the Mugodzhary Hills—descends due south toward the Aral Sea.

However, most of the Turanian Lowlands are low and flat. But east of the Turgai River Valley gradually rises a predominantly flat, immense plateau, occupying most of Central Asia's northeastern quarter.

In Central Asia's southeastern quarter the rising country forms foothill areas. These swell into a broad, massive, mountainous region with great ice-capped ranges. In these mountains lie part of the Uzbek and all of the Tadzhik and Kirghiz SSR's.

Most of Central Asia has one cardinal problem—water. Except for limited areas, the huge country always lacks water.

Winters are cold, for blasts of icy wind blow across Siberia from the Arctic, and summers are long and very hot. The mercury rises to 112° F. almost anywhere in Central Asia, while in Termez (in Southern Uzbekistan) it shoots up to 122° F.

Proceeding from north to south, Central Asia may be divided into four belts or zones.

First are the fertile black and chestnut soils extending from Western Siberia into Northern Kazakhstan which form its northern unirrigated agriculture belt. Its southernmost provinces are those of Uralsk, Ak-

tyubinsk, Semipalatinsk; its main center is Tselinograd (former Ak-
molinsk).

Formerly the land was used mainly for cattle breeding because
of its dryness. However, in the 1950's, the Soviet Government felt
that more grain fields were needed and about 50 million acres of
Northern Kazakhstan's virgin steppe were turned into fields, mainly
for wheat.

Thus, Northern Kazahkstan's farming has become quite important
to the general Soviet food production, though occasionally droughts
occur in the region. Its population has greatly increased, swollen by
the inflow of volunteers who came from all over Russia to break the
soil. Its cities have grown tremendously. Their growth has been also
due to the region's industrialization. During the years of Joseph Stalin's
rule, the Soviet Government sent a multitude of convict laborers to
work in Kazakhstan's numerous new coal, copper, iron ore, and other
mines.

The second belt is that of semi-deserts and deserts of various types
—clays, sand, wormwood, and saline. It covers 60 percent of Kazakhstan, 80 percent of Turkmenistan, and about half of Uzbekistan, plus
desert areas scattered elsewhere. Dwellers of these various deserts
have always been nomadic and mainly bred domestic animals. Lately,
however, the majority have settled down.

In spring, most of Central Asia's deserts produce a carpet of lush
green grass and bright flowers, and become excellent pastures. But
as summer wears on the blindingly sunlit desert becomes brownish-

yellow. Rivers dry up, some ending in a brackish water swamp, or in a chain of stagnant puddles. Watering animals becomes a problem. Most collective animal farms send their sheep and cattle to the uplands, where vegetation burns out later, and finally to high mountain pastures.

In some areas, especially in Kazakhstan and Turkmenistan, a camel caravan, or a donkey drawing a heavily laden cart with two wheels the height of a man may still be seen (though the motor truck is increasingly replacing the camel). The herdsman and his family still live in the same kind of a *yúrta* (a tent made of a light wooden frame, covered with felt and transported on a camel's hump) as that which his forefathers lived in under Ghengis Khan.

Central Asia's great mineral wealth lies largely in this belt. Nature has concealed under the yellowish-brown, sun-scorched soil two important oil regions (one in Kazakhstan, the other in Turkmenistan), as well as natural gas, copper, manganese, gold, and other mineral deposits which are now being exploited.

The third belt is that of the oases. These are found scattered in desert stretches wherever there is water. The country's largest, almost continuous and most important oasis is the erratically broken-up foothill belt. This consists of well-watered areas such as the valleys between the plain and the great mountains in the south and southeast.

In contrast to the rude and primitive nomads of the desert, the people of the oases have always been settled farmers, gardeners, and fruit-growers.

Not only Mohammedan, but also much earlier cultures have developed, struggled, and bloomed here. Persians, Greeks, Arabs, Tartar-Mongols collided in the area. Elaborate systems of irrigation, much older than ours, were set up in the land, and agriculture flourished. Important trade routes crossed the foothill belt, including the Chinese "silk road" to the Near East and Europe. Before the beginning of our era cities of antiquity sprang up, such as Marghelan, Tashkent, Samarkand, Osh, Andizhan, Bukhara, and Merv (now Mary).

Samarkand, then called *Marakand*, was especially famed. In the fourth century B.C. the Persian Emperor Cyrus, and later Alexander the Great, fought for it. In the fourteenth and fifteenth centuries, Tamerlane made Samarkand capital of his far-flung empire. Arts, philosophy, and sciences flourished in it then. Mirroring the age in which they had been built, Tamerlane's Tomb and Samarkand's mosques and *medresséhs* (theological schools), which have survived subsequent centuries of Central Asia's decline, have few equals for originality and majestic beauty.

With the development of maritime traffic, Central Asia lost its role as the main connecting link between the Far East and Europe. It split into small, despotic Moslem principalities and hordes, which fought among themselves and raided Russia's border regions.

The submission of Kazakh hordes to Russia, begun in the eighteenth century, was completed in 1865. Between 1868 and 1876 Russia also annexed—after but a few real battles—the last independent States in the present-day Uzbekistan: the Khanates of Khivá and of Kokand and the Ameerate of Bokhará. The Khan of Khivá and the Ameer of Bokhará remained, however, hereditary rulers of their principalities, vassal to the Tsar. Like the Tsar, they were dethroned only by the Revolution of 1917.

After the Revolution a large-scale guerrilla warfare against the Soviet regime broke out in Central Asia, especially in the south. Warfare went on for years but was finally quelled in 1925.

At present the majority of Central Asia's population still lives as always in the foothill belt and in the oases. Thus, in Uzbekistan are the most densely peopled areas of the entire Soviet Union, with over thousand inhabitants per square mile. However, in the nearby desert zone of that same republic, a square mile counts eight to fourteen dwellers.

Here, too, Central Asia produces the bulk of cotton, rice, fruit, melons, grapes, and other farm products which it contributes to the Soviet economy. Numerous mining developments and most of the country's large industrial cities are located in the foothill belt. One of its main links is the Ferganá Valley, lying 100 miles east of Tashkent, and known since antiquity as "Central Asia's pearl." Three different sections of it belong to three neighboring republics—the Uzbek, Tadzhik, and Kirghiz SSR's. It combines a great mineral wealth with rare agricultural wealth.

The Valley is only about two hundred miles long and eighty miles wide but is protected from the northern winds by mountains. It grows 60 percent of all cotton produced by the Uzbek SSR. The Valley's ancient irrigation system using small streams coming down the mountainsides was highly improved by the completion, in 1939, of the Great Ferghana Canal.

The foothill belt is served best by railroads. The Transcaspian Railroad, the bulk of which was completed in 1888, runs the length of the entire belt and connects most of its important cities. With the construction of that first competitor to the camel caravan, Central Asia's modern economic development began. Later, railroads running from the north, across Kazakhstan, to the Transcaspian have been added to it. Central Asia's automobile road network, also oriented toward the foothill belt, is well developed.

The fourth zone of Central Asia are its mountains running along the southern and the eastern edge of the country and occupying the bulk of its southeastern quarter. These mountains form several ranges. The Pamir Plateau (or "Roof of the World") is a plateau 14,000 feet high, where Russia borders on Afghanistan and on Sinkiang. Marco Polo was the first one to visit it shortly after 1271 and described its wild and mysterious beauty. The moisture-free air of the Plateau has a crystalline transparency which allows one to see for miles.

The great Pamir-Alay Ranges also rise on that plateau and fan out northwestward. In the northeast they are confined by the Trans-Alay (*Zaalaiskiy*) Range. All of these are among the highest in the world. They count peaks, such as Mt. Communism (24,590 feet) or Mt. Lenin (23,405), which dwarf those of the Caucasus. North of the Trans-Alay Range is a system of ranges called the Tyan-Shan. These reach into Sinkiang.

Between the northernmost spur of the Tyan-Shans and parallel mountains 140 miles to the north is a relatively flat terrain known as the Dzhungarian Gate. Through that Gate, offering convenient routes from China westward, marched many an invader in far-off centuries, to Central Asia and from there to South Russia's steppes and Europe.

On the Pamir Plateau and on high mountain slopes the population is sparse. There are chiefly Kirghiz and Tadzhik herdsmen roaming over rich Alpine pastures with sheep, horses, cattle, and living in their felt-covered tents. They often wear their old national costume: a

quilted gown, soft boots, and a felt hat banded around with fur flaps.

Scarcity of forests is one of Central Asia's typical features. Not even the Pamir-Alays and the Tyan-Shans are very rich in them. At the altitude of 6,300 to 10,000 feet there is some vegetation: first, thickets of briar and honeysuckle, then maple, walnut, damson, apple, apricot, and wild almond woods, and still nearer the upper limit slender Tyan-Shan pines and silver firs. However, these wooded patches do not match the impenetrable forests on Caucasian mountain slopes.

Most of Central Asian rivers rise in the glaciers and snow fields of its great ranges, or of the Hindu Kush, on the Afghan side of the border. The two largest and most important rivers are the Amu-Darya (better known to the Westerners as the Oxus) and the Syr-Darya. Smaller rivers—such as the Tedzhen, the Murgab, the Zeravshan—are born in these ranges also. Reaching no sea or lake, they just dry up in the sands. However, they are quite important to irrigation. Thus the Zeravshan, in Uzbekistan, has been for unnumbered centuries a cradle of Central Asiatic civilizations. Before expiring, it feeds its waters to the blooming oasis, some 200 miles long, where Samarkand and Bukhará are found.

The Kazakh SSR.   As nomads, the Kazakhs were long divided into three hordes—the Great, Medium, and Small hordes. War with their stronger neighbors prompted the Medium and Small hordes to seek the protection of Empress Anne of Russia in 1730. Part of the Great Horde passed under the Russian rule in 1819; the rest in 1865.

The Kazakhs enjoyed a feudal self-government until 1917. They had their own elected *khans* (rulers), confirmed by the Russian Government. After the Revolution Kazakhstan became first an autonomous republic of the RSFSR, and in 1936 a union republic.

Ural Cossacks have migrated to Northern Kazakhstan since the seventeenth century. Some of its main present-day cities—Petropavlovsk, Semipalatinsk, and Ust-Kamenogorsk—were at first tiny Cossack fortresses. In the 1900's, Russian peasants from overpopulated areas flocked there, but the inflow of Russians and Ukrainians into Kazakhstan increased especially under the Soviets.

At present, out of its 12,130,000 inhabitants, only 30 percent are Kazakhs. Fifteen percent are of other Central Asiatic nationalities, chiefly Uzbeks. Russians account for 42 percent of the population,

Ukrainians for 8 percent, and Belorussians for 1 percent. Most Russians and Ukranians live in the northern belt, in the larger cities and industrial centers.

Alma-Ata, which means in Kazakh "Father of Apples," is Kazakhstan's capital. It was founded by Russians as a fortress and garrison city in 1854 and named Verniy (Loyal). Situated 2,800 feet above ocean level, in the foothills of the Tyan-Shans, it has a reputation as one of the loveliest of Soviet cities. Snowcapped peaks and forest-covered slopes serve as Alma-Ata's backdrop; in the city itself are broad asphalt avenues lined with poplars and a profusion of orchards and parks. Alma-Ata has now 650,000 inhabitants. It is a fast-growing city but its misfortune is that severe earthquakes occur in the area.

Besides heavy machine-building, Alma-Ata specializes in processing local produce—in cotton-spinning, fruit-canning, meat-packing, leather-tanning, shoe and cloth industries.

Chimkent, 300 miles west of Alma-Ata, is an important lead-and zinc-smelting center. The low Karadag Range nearby contains large deposits of polymetallic ores.

North of Kazakhstan's foothill fringe are some of the country's most desolate deserts. Here are the Muyunkum Sands and the *Bet-Pak-Dalá* (or Hungary Steppe) with a cracked clay and salt crust, famed for its mirages which deceive the traveler with sights of magnificent, shady trees and streams where there are none.

Nearby is Lake Balkhash, which is quite narrow but some 330 miles long. Its western half, fed by the Ili River, has virtually fresh water, in contrast to its saltwater eastern half.

Besides small fishing settlements, the Kounrad copper ore deposits, rating among the richest in the Soviet Union, lie along the lake's northern shore. Two other important copper ore deposits are also part of this area. Together, the three contain more than half of the Soviet Union's known copper reserves.

The city of Karaganda is a large center of heavy industries and of an important coal basin developed chiefly by convict labor under Stalin. This and the newborn city of Temirtau form the heart of the mining areas. Temirtau has iron and steel works serving the region, as well as a coke-chemical plant. Karaganda makes the mining equipment needed.

Kazakhstan's easternmost corner—the area of Ust-Kamenogorsk and Leninogorsk—has very large polymetallic ore deposits. Lying on the spurs of the Siberian Altay Mountains, this is also a good agricultural area with dairies, herds of Siberian stag, and fields of wheat. All of northeastern Kazakhstan is crossed diagonally, southeast-to-northwest, by the large Irtysh River.

Around Ust-Kamenogorsk are two large hydroelectric power plants on this river, and the Soviets are now carrying out a grand-scale water-supply project here.

West of this area is the little port and city of Aralsk, on the Aral Sea. Like the Caspian, the Aral is an inland sea. Lying in the middle of the Turanian Lowlands, it is confined by flat, treeless, burnt-out shores. The land has little rain. It is a blindingly sunlit desert with an occasional camel caravan and a few fishing settlements set far apart. The Aral Sea, bluish-green, shallow, strewn with islands, is comparatively rich in fish. There are some fish-processing and canning plants nearby, the largest one in Aralsk. This city also has ship-repair yards.

Some collective farms in the area engage in camel breeding. The Novokazalinsk and the Kzyl-Ordá oases grow a great deal of rice. Kzyl-Ordá is a food-processing center. The reed thickets along the river are used for the manufacture of pulp and cardboard; they also harbor the tiger, which inhabits Central Asia's swampy and wooded places.

Between the Aral and the middle part of the Caspian shores lie the Ust-Yurt Uplands, a desklike plateau of clay and stone at the height of a few hundred feet. This descends to the Aral shore and the plain in an abrupt, sheer cliff. All but waterless, it is virtually uninhabited.

To the northwest is the Caspian Depression encompassing, in a broad band, the northern part of the Caspian Sea. That sea is slowly drying up and even now lies 86 feet below ocean level. In these low-lying sand-and-salt stretches between the Ural and Emba rivers are scattered hundreds of oil-bearing salt cupolas. This is the important Ural-Emba oil and natural gas region.

Exploitation of the Emba fields began in 1911. Lately it has been considerably expanded and it is now scattered over an area about 250 miles long. In the estuary of the Ural River the port of Guriev is the Emba Region's headquarters and refining center. Another refinery is located in the Ural Region. Oil is conveyed to it from Guriev by a 430-mile pipeline. Guriev is also a fishing port on the Caspian Sea and has the largest fish cannery in Kazakhstan, as well as nurseries for the valuable species of fish.

The Turkmen SSR is more than twice as large as Italy, but Italy's population is twenty-seven times that of Turkmenistan. Over 80 percent of the area belongs to the Kara-Kum Desert, the largest single sand desert in Central Asia. Turkmenistan is the thirstiest of the Central Asiatic countries and only 1 percent of its land is cultivated.

Turkmenistan's scant population lives chiefly in its narrow fringes: in the comparatively well-watered southern foothills of the low Kopet Dag Range; along the Transcaspian Railroad; along the water-rich Amu-Darya River framing the country from the east; and in the oases along the Tedzhen and Murgab rivers which cut into the desert from the south.

Turkmenistan's native inhabitants, the Turkmens, form 61 percent of its total population. The rest are Russians, Uzbeks, Kazakhs, Tartars, Ukrainians, and Armenians.

Turkmens are closely related to the Osmanli Turks (inhapitants of Turkey) and to the Azerbaidzhanians. Warlike nomads, they roamed the desert for centuries with their sheep and cattle, raiding Russian caravans or Uzbek cities.

In the first half of the nineteenth century, hard pressed by Uzbek khanates, some Turkmen tribes sought Russian protection. By the end of the century Russia had annexed the whole country.

The Kara-Kum (or Black Sands) Desert looks like a sea, with long, high waves of sand and a delicate pattern of ripples drawn on them by wind. Whole stretches of it are covered with tufts of coarse prickly grass, wormwood or "sand reeds." It is a grazing ground, especially for sheep. Even though the amount of fodder is small, the desert's endless expanse leaves space for many animals. Water is provided by over 10,000 wells. Among the Kara-Kum's dwellers are lizards and snakes, including the deadly cobra. There are also thickets of *saxaul*, a desert tree with tiny scales instead of leaves, providing no shade. Storms are dangerous when whirling sand, as thin as powder, gets into one's mouth, eyes, nostrils. Many a caravan perished here.

Turkmenistan supplies the Soviets with 20 percent of their exportable caracul pelts. Excellent horses also come from this region and there is some camel breeding.

In the oases there is irrigated agriculture. Turkmenistan is an important Soviet producer of cotton. Melon fields, vineyards, truck gardens, and some wheat are grown. Silkworm breeding and bee-keeping are also popular. Subsoil waters in the Kopet Dag foothills are collected, for irrigation, in the underground galleries, some a few miles long.

Turkmenistan's largest irrigation project is the Kara-Kum Canal, completed in 1962. This is probably the largest of its kind in the world. Branching out from the upper Amu-Darya, in the country's southeastern corner, it carries part of its water 480 miles due west, to Ashkhabad. It boosts the water resources of the Murgab and Tedzhen oases which it crosses and abundantly supplies with water the Ashkhabad area. The canal has reclaimed some 500,000 acres for farming. It is navigable by light motor craft.

Set in front of the spectacular range of the Kopet Dags is Ashkhabad, Turkmenistan's capital, main cultural center, and largest industrial city. Full of modern, showy official buildings, it is neat, attractive, and rich in greenery. It is something of a Soviet Hollywood: many Soviet films have been made there. In its streets and bazaars Western clothes mix with old Moslem embroidered skullcaps and long *khalats*.

Other Turkmen cities are small. About 200 miles east of the capital is the city of Mary, formerly called Merv. The present city was founded by Russians in 1884 and is a junction of the Transcaspian Railroad. It has a cotton spinnery and a large wool-washery. A few miles east are the remainders of the old Merv, which was a great metropolis of the ancient world. It was first mentioned in the year 1200 B.C.

The Mary Province is a producer of the lovely and highly valued Turkmen rugs. These are made by Turkmen women, often in a nomad's tent. The craft is passed on from mothers to daughters.

Bairam-Ali, near Mary; Chardzhow, in a famed melon-growing area on the Amu-Darya River; and Tashauz on its lower reaches are the only significant cities in Eastern Turkmenistan. They all engage chiefly in the processing of local raw materials. Chardzhow is the largest and has the only plant for the dressing of caracul pelts in Turkmenistan.

Near Bairam-Ali large deposits of natural gas have been found, which is pipelined via Saratov on the Volga to the Moscow region.

The main city in Western Turkmenistan is Krasnovodsk. It is the country's only important Caspian Sea port and is the starting point of the Transcaspian Railroad. The city is an oil-refining center, for near it the important Nebit-Dag oil region lies.

Drab little Krasnovodsk sits at the foot of a steep cliff, above which lies the flat Krasnovodsk Plateau. The city gets drinking water from Caspian tankers. Besides the refinery, it has a fish-processing combine and ship-repair yards.

North of it lies Kara-Bogaz-Gol, a large, shallow gulf, joined to the Caspian by a very narrow strait. Evaporating much quicker than in the open sea, water here becomes a concentrated solution of various salts. They pile up in mounds of white crystals along the shore. Out of these deposits, Glauber's salt, used in medicine and in chemical industries, is extracted.

The Uzbek SSR is by far the richest, most advanced, and most populous of Central Asia's four southern republics. Though not quite as large as Turkmenistan, it has 10,581,000 inhabitants. Tashkent, its capital, is the largest Soviet city east of the Volga Region and the Caucasus. Uzbekistan combines Moslem medievalism with a pronounced industrial development.

Uzbeks form 63 percent of the republic's population. The rest are Russians, who live chiefly in cities, Tadzhiks, Kazakhs, Tartars and other Central Asiatic peoples.

Who are Uzbeks? In 1312–40, Khan *Uzbek* ruled over the Golden Horde. After his death some Turk and Mongol tribes which had been among his subjects began to call themselves Uzbeks.

Uzbekistan is favorably situated. The area is rich in rivers and was at one time irrigated by a number of ditches and 70,000 ancient water-raising wheels. Now old irrigation systems are being boosted by effective new ones, with large concrete dams, electric pumps, and controlled distribution of water.

Uzbekistan produces two-thirds of all cotton harvested in Russia. "Cotton is a child of the sun," Uzbeks say. "It likes to stand with its feet in the water and its head in the sun." In Uzbek oases both water and sun are plentiful. Uzbekistan also produces many crops, such as wheat, fruit, and rice, and is rich in minerals.

Tashkent is Uzbekistan's capital, Central Asia's main industrial city, and a busy metropolis. Known since the seventeenth century, it was the seat of the Russian General-governorship of Turkestan from 1871 to 1917. That, and its central position, accounted for its initial growth. In 1871 it had 78,000 inhabitants; now it has 1,140,000.

Tashkent has the largest textile combine in Central Asia. It produces all of the cotton-picking machines and half of the spinning frames made in Russia. It builds general machinery and engages in food, leather goods, and other industries. The city is the seat of the Grand Muftí, or spiritual leader of Central Asia's Moslems.

A peculiar sight in Tashkent are irrigation *aryks,* neatly dug along the streets beside the pavement, often cemented, usually lined with trees. Fed by the Chirchik River, the *aryks* keep Tashkent's numerous gardens and parks luxuriant. In the "Old Town," one still sees some flat-roofed clay Moslem homes, with no windows facing the street. Picturesque also are Tashkent's bazaars with their Oriental crowds and especially the cafes where men in skullcaps or turbans and *khalats* eat the pilau of rice, lamb, and *uryuk* (dried apricots) or, stroking their beards, play chess.

Tashkent has a very busy airport for it lies astride the air routes leading from European Russia to the Far East, India, Afghanistan, and China.

This is also an important industrial region, for on the Chirchik and the Angren rivers is a "cascade" of hydroelectric power plants.

East of Tashkent are some new industrial developments. The city of Chirchik has an electrochemical combine producing fertilizer for cotton fields. Farther south there are a coal-mining region, vast poly-metallic ore deposits, and a copper refinery; and steel mills at Begovat —the only ones in Central Asia's southern republics.

Near Begovat lies what used to be the waterless "Starvation Steppe." Now, because of the Northern and the Southern Starvation Steppe Canals, this is a great cotton-growing region.

South of Tashkent, a spur line leads off the Transcaspian Railroad eastward into the Fergana Valley ("Central Asia's Pearl"). In the city of Fergana there is a large oil refinery. Amidst cotton fields and orchards heavy with fruit, numerous oil derricks can be seen in the Valley, especially near Andizhan.

In the Zeravshan Oasis, Samarkand—with its monuments of the past, modern university, and other educational institutions—is an Uzbek cultural center second to Tashkent alone. Among its industries, spare parts for tractors and cinematographic equipment are made. In the same oasis sits Bukhara, also an ancient city permeated with history.

At Gazli, near Boukhara, and at Uch-Kyr, near the Aral Sea, large natural gas deposits were discovered. Together with similar deposits in Turkmenistan, at Bairam-Ali, they feed two great pipelines which carry gas to cities thousands of miles away.

The northern third of Uzbekistan holds the *Kara-Kalpak Autonomous SSR,* bordering on the southern half of the Aral Sea.

Its total population is 620,000; a third of them are Kara-Kalpaks, or "Black Bonnets," so named because black caracul caps are their historical headgear. They speak a Turkic language and are closely related to the Kirghiz and Kazakhs.

This republic is Uzbekistan's poorest and most backward region. Until recently, nearly all of its population was illiterate. Most of the country lies on the barren, dismal Ust-Yurt Plateau which descends to the sea in almost vertical cliffs, a few hundred feet high. The republic's only fertile lands lie along the Amu-Darya's lower course in the Khorezm Oasis. Oasis agriculture, sheep breeding, and fishing, are the Kara-Kalpaks' main pursuits. The republic's capital is Nukus, with a population of 53,000.

The Tadzhik SSR is the smallest of the Central Asiatic republics, about equal to the states of New York and Connecticut combined.

Instead of plains and deserts Tadzhikistan is filled with impressive mountains, for over half of it lies above the altitude of 6,560 feet. Of course there are small foothill areas as well, 1,000 to 1,500 feet high, which include many valleys and oases. In these places live most of Tadzhikistan's 2,579,000 people. Fifty-three percent of them are Tadzhiks and among the others are Uzbeks, Russians, and Kirghiz.

The Tadzhiks, Iranian by origin and language, are Central Asia's earliest inhabitants. They are softer and more imaginative than the firm, strong-willed Uzbeks. Their ancestors have lived in this vicinity since the beginning of the first millennium B.C. The tenth to eleventh centuries were the Tadzhiks' Golden Age. Treatises by Avicenna, a Tadzhik thinker, served until the 1600's as the guide of medical study in European universities.

Protected from winds, Tadzhikistan's narrow, warm valleys are planted with the usual crops of Central Asia, plus some citrus fruit. The main features of the landscape are irrigation *aryks;* fields white with cotton bursting out of ripe bolls; Tadzhik girls in white *khalats* (gowns) or cotton-picking machines at work.

A large dam, built on the mighty, turbulent Syr-Darya River as it emerges from the Fergana Valley, produced the huge "Tadzhik or Kayra-Kum Sea" in 1959. Two large-capacity hydroelectric power plants are located here and the "Sea" helps to irrigate the surrounding area.

Dushanbé (327,000), Tadzhikistan's capital, sits in the Ghissar

Valley. The city has existed only since 1925; before that it was a village located at major crossroads which are now automobile roads. Attractively adorned with parks and a large lake, Dushanbé produces automatic looms and has a textile combine, a tanning and shoe plant, and a cement works. A railroad connects it with the Transcaspian.

The only other sizeable city in Tadzhikistan is Leninabad, which sits in an oasis by the "Tadzhik Sea." Its chief function is the processing of local farm produce.

Tadzhikistan's southern part is an autonomous unit—*Gorno-Badakhshan Autonomous District*—occupying the entire Pamir Plateau.

The Pamir forms 43 percent of Tadzhikistan's territory but only 4 percent of the republic's population inhabit that rugged plateau. In the west, gouged out by turbulent tributaries of the Pyandzh, the plateau is accessible. Farming is possible in these river gorges. Cabbages, potatoes, mulberry trees are grown, and patches of soil are sown to wheat or millet. The stone huts of Tadzhik mountaineers nestle in the rocks.

But the Pamir's central and eastern sections are forbidding. The wide base of the valleys lies at an altitude of over 13,000 feet. Masses of ice and snow tower over some of them. The mountain air is rarified. Among Pamir's wild animals are *archars*, large mountain sheep with twisted antlers, which were hunted by President Theodore Roosevelt.

Eastern Pamir is peopled mostly by Kirghiz herdsmen roaming with their sheep and yaks. The animals graze all year round on sweeps of grassy uplands, strewn with boulders, between the ranges. There is no snow in winter, although it piles up two or three yards high down below. The great Pamir ranges shut off all moist winds from the middle terrain.

The AD's administrative center is the village of Khorg (11,000) on the Pyandzh River which borders Afghanistan. There are no railways on the Pamir but important automobile roads radiate from Khorg.

The Kirghiz SSR is one-third larger than Tadzhikistan and just as mountainous.

Nearly half of Kirghizia lies 9,800 or more feet above ocean level. Only in the north, in the valleys of the Chu and the Talass rivers and in the Kirghiz portion of the Fergana Valley, are there stretches no higher than 1,600 to 3,100 feet.

The country's population is 2,652,000. The Kirghiz, with their broad, flattish faces, form only 40 percent of it, however. The rest of the inhabitants are Russians, Ukrainians, Uzbeks, Dungans (Moslem Chinese from Sinkiang), and others. Among the Russians, Ukrainians, and other small groups there are numerous deportees of Stalin's times. In mountain valleys south of Frunze, there were—or still are—settlements of banished Volga Germans, Chechens, and Ingushes.

Kirghiz nomads—chiefly sheep and horse breeders—have been in the Tyan-Shans since the first century B.C. Many of them are Moslems, with a mixture of Shamanist beliefs.

Most of Kirghizia's ranges, belonging to the Tyan-Shan system, are oriented west-to-east. Among the snow- and ice-capped peaks of the Kokshaal-Tau—highest of these ranges—are Mt. Pobedy (Peak of Victory), 24,406 feet, and Mt. Khan-Tengri, 22,940 feet. They rear their glistening heads in the northeast, near Sinkiang's border.

About 100 miles west of these summits, at an altitude of 5,279 feet, lies Lake Issyk-Kul. This is Kirghizia's largest lake. Its blue, brackish waters reflect the two great northern and southern ranges which confine it. Thirty miles off its northern shore, Kazakhstan's sands stretch far away. Ships and fishing boats ply the lake. In Kirghiz, *issyk-kul* means "warm lake." It never freezes, for there are hot, radioactive springs around it, and health resorts have grown up nearby. At its western tip is the little Rybacheye, its main port and city. At the lake's opposite end, in the port of Przhevalsk, stands an impressive monument to Nikolai Przhevalsky, great Russian explorer of Central Asia and discoverer of Przhevalsky's horse, a wild horse intermediate between true horses and asses, who died there in 1888.

Kirghizia produces nearly enough food and fodder grains—chiefly wheat and corn—for its own needs. In the Chu River Valley with its irrigation network, sugar beets are grown for the six sugar refineries. Kenaf, tobacco, and large medicinal poppy plantations give bright color to the lakeshore plain. There is much livestock breeding and the endless mountain pastures are one of the country's assets.

Forty percent of the coal mined in Central Asia's southern republics comes from Kirghizia. The Tyan-Shans yield mercury, lead, much antimony and—in the Kirghiz part of the Fergana Valley—oil and gas.

Overlooking the Chu River Valley with its wheat and sugar beet fields, Frunze (Pishpek), the capital, with 385,000 inhabitants, is attractively situated. Its chief industries are farm-machinery construction, food processing, and textiles. Soon the first automobile assembly plant in southern Central Asia will start functioning there.

Kirghizia's only other largish city is Osh, in the Fergana Valley. Its inhabitants work chiefly at its silk combine, cotton-cleaning mill, and food concerns. Osh is one of Central Asia's oldest cities. It straddles the old caravan route to China and it still remains an important communication center.

IO

★

THE URALS, SIBERIA, AND THE FAR EAST

In quest of valuable furs, twelfth-century Russians from Novgorod penetrated into the stern, northern, sparsely peopled land between the upper Kama River and the Ural Mountains. Two hundred and fifty years later, their pioneering yielded unexpected results.

In the 1580's, the Stroganovs, a wealthy Novgorod family, possessed immense landed estates in the Kama-Urals area. However, they were often raided by local tribes and even by Tartars of Khan Kuchum from beyond the Urals.

Ivan the Terrible, then Tsar of Muscovy, allowed the Stroganovs to fortify their towns and keep their own troops in their domains. He even urged them to set up fortified points east of the mountains.

The Stroganovs hired Yermak Timofeyevich, a Cossack chieftain, with a troop of 540, and added 300 men of their own.

In 1581, Yermak launched his campaign. East of the Urals his "army" sailed in boats down smaller rivers toward the Irtysh River, on which sat *Sibir* (Siberia), the Khan's capital. Twice he defeated Kuchum's forces and occupied Sibir. Elated, Ivan annexed the conquered khanate and sent rich gifts to Yermak and the Strogonovs.

A historical task was accomplished, for the immense land beyond the Urals—nearly twice as large as the United States—was all but empty. The peoples inhabiting it were trappers, fishermen, and reindeer herdsmen. Their tribes were scattered and their princelings disunited. It took the Muscovites only sixty years to become masters of that huge land and emerge on the Pacific shore.

The tsars accomplished this by barter, diplomacy, and town building rather than by fighting. The Russians advanced eastward chiefly along the great land's southern fringe, where forests give way to steppe and where, 350 years in the future, the Trans-Siberian Railroad would pass. They also advanced northward, down Siberia's mighty rivers. Their eastward progress was marked by the building of fortified towns. Such, for instance, were Tyumen (founded in 1586), Tobolsk (1587), Tomsk (1604), Krasnoyarsk (1628), and many others. Okhotsk, first Russian port on the Pacific shore, appeared in 1649.

These towns were primitive, made up of log cabins and a church, encompassed by a solid wooden fence. They served the purpose of withstanding raids and offering shelter from the severe cold of the Siberian winter. Now most of them are large economic and cultural centers with industrial plants, cinemas, theaters, airports, and universities.

This area has proven to be very rich, primarily in valuable furs (the earliest Russian pioneer was the trapper), in mineral resources from iron, copper, lead, bauxites, rare metals, and fabulous amounts of coal to gold, silver, platinum, diamonds; rich in timber (the forests of Eastern Siberia alone exceeded by 50 percent those of all Europe), and in fish.

The economic development of the Urals yielded large results even in the eighteenth century. But, due to the length and difficulty of communications, Siberia and the Far East's initial progress was slow. The Trans-Siberian Railroad, completed partially in 1897 and fully in 1916, aided their development enormously.

Excluding the Ural Region proper, the endless land east of it still has a population of but 24,606,000, or that of the states of New York and Michigan combined. Along the Trans-Siberian Railroad and at some points along the rivers, there are important and rapidly growing industrial areas and clusters of population. But north of the railroad, between the rivers, remain hundreds of thousands of square miles of unexplored taiga and tundra.

The Soviets are trying hard to step up the tempo of the great land's development. Their efforts yield results. Siberia is playing an increasingly important role in Russia's general life. And many regard it as a land of the future—as "Russia's America."

The Ural Region. This region takes its name from the Ural Mountains which run south from the icy shores of the Kara Sea to Kazakhstan's scorching steppes, about 1,200 miles away.

The Urals are low, very old, worn-out mountains; Narodnaya Gora (or People's Mountain), the loftiest peak located in the north, is 6,183 feet high; their average altitude is about 1,600 feet.

The Northern Urals form one comparatively high range, stony and craggy, which slopes down to the east more steeply than to the west. The Middle Urals split into three and four lower and less distinctly outlined parallel chains. The Southern section fans out into ten to twelve ranges or mountain masses, some higher than the Middle Urals, with deep river valleys in between.

The Urals' watershed range divides the Kama River's drainage basin in the west from that of the Ob and the Irtysh in the east. It also serves as the dividing line between Europe and Asia.

The Ural Region here comprises only the Middle and the Southern Ural Mountains. It is an irregularly shaped territory, some 10 percent larger than Texas, about 660 miles long north to south, with a western border of wide, rolling plains and flat lowlands in the east.

The Urals' climate is continental. Winters are cold. Frosts of —40° F., and in the northeast even —52° F., are usual. They are bearable only because there is no wind. Only in the south are there severe snowstorms. The summer is mild even in the north, with the July temperature averaging 62° F.

Except for a belt of steppe in the south, the region is heavily forested. On the Urals' eastern slopes pine prevails, and on the western ones, reached by humid winds, spruce and fir. In the middle Urals there are large expanses of cedar and larch trees, found growing all over Siberia. In the south, oak, maple, elm, and linden are prevalent.

Especially in their eastern slopes, the old, worn-out Ural Mountains hold a fabulous mineral wealth. The region's 12,000 known deposits contain nearly every useful or valuable mineral our planet has produced.

Therefore, the Urals are one of the main Soviet industrial areas. They are an agricultural region as well. The southern provinces of Orenburg, Chelyabinsk, and Kurgan, are an important wheat-growing and cattle-breeding land, fusing with the Northern Kazakhstan.

The Urals' total population is 15,634,000. A great majority of these are Russians with some Ukrainians. The region's ancient original dwellers—the Udmurts, Komi-Permyaks, and Mansis of the Finno-Ugric group—make up only about 4 percent of that figure.

As a result of the impetus given to the development of the Urals by Peter the Great in the eighteenth century, about one hundred small blast furnaces burning charcoal belched smoke in their wooded hills. Since the 1860's, however, the leading role in Russia's ferrous metallurgy passed to much more modern plants in the centrally located Ukraine.

In 1929, the Soviet Government decided to transform the Urals into "the Soviet Union's second metallurgical base." New mines were sunk and large new concerns, from steel mills, copper or zinc smelters, and aluminum works to tractor, armament, aircraft, and various other plants, were built or old ones modernized at a rapid tempo. This plan has paid off; in particular, during World War II, the Ural plants gave the Soviet armies 40 per cent of all their armaments.

The region's main city is Sverdlovsk (940,000), formerly called Ekaterinburg. Peter the Great founded it in 1721 as a fortress and headquarters of the Urals' iron works. It sits in a picturesque country of wooded hills and lakes.

The city's past is marred by somber tragedy, for in 1918 ex-Emperor Nicholas II, his wife Alexandra, and their five children—all of them helpless prisoners of the Bolsheviks (Communists)—were massacred by their jailers in Ekaterinburg.

Sverdlovsk is a great industrial center. Especially important are its plants producing electrical machinery, excavators, heavy drilling equipment, and equipment for chemical plants. East of the city sits the Beloyarskaya Atomic Power Plant.

Around Sverdlovsk are some of the Ural's main copper mines and smelting centers. Gold, diamonds, and asbestos are mined east of the city. North of it, Nizhniy Taghil, the Sverdlovsk Province's main metallurgical center, dating back to 1725, sits amidst iron ore deposits.

Chelyabinsk is the region's second-largest city and the starting point of the Trans-Siberian Railroad. As an idustrial city it is particularly well known in the Soviet Union for its mammoth tractor plant.

Both Sverdlovsk and Chelyabinsk are located on the Siberian side of the Ural Ranges. Perm, on the European side, occupies a 25-mile-long stretch on the elevated bank of the Kama River. Among its main industrial features is a large oil refinery, for some of the fields of the

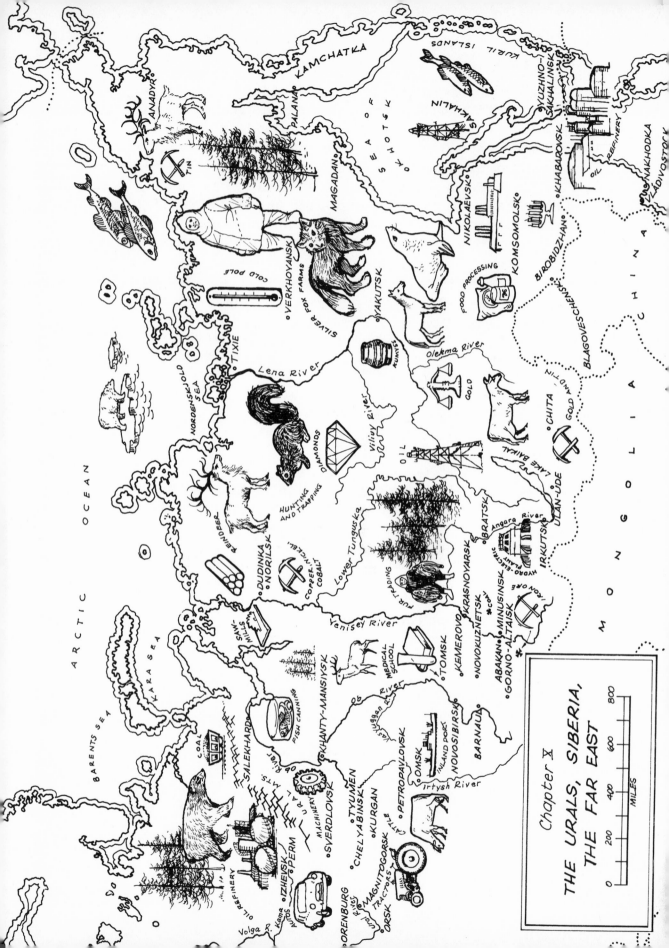

Chapter X

THE URALS, SIBERIA,
THE FAR EAST

Volga-Urals Oil Region are nearby. Tracing its history back to the seventeenth century, Perm has long been the Urals' leading cultural center.

In the northeastern corner of the Perm Province lies the tiny *Komi-Permyak National District*. The Komi-Permyaks form about half of the 220,000 population. They belong to the Finno-Urgic group and are closely related to the inhabitants of the Komi ASSR. This is a primitive, heavily wooded area, and the Komi-Permyaks engage chiefly in the timber industry.

More important is the *Udmurt ASSR*, west of the Perm Province. Of its 1,375,000 inhabitants, 485,000 are Udmurts, also of the Finnish group. Their tongue—and their little country—resemble those of the Komis.

Izhevsk (360,000), Udmurtia's main city, is an important machine-building, woodworking, and food-processing center. The city's pride is a large new motorcar plant.

Most of the Urals' cities mentioned so far were built in 1721–42. But in Soviet times new ones have mushroomed up.

The principal of these is Magnitogorsk (352,000) built on the Ural River southwest of Chelyabinsk and framed by orchards. It is famed for its foundry and steel mills, put up with American technical assistance and said to be the largest in the world. The city's name derives from Magnitnaya Mountain rising beside it.

Magnitogorsk was founded in 1929 as "living quarters" for the builders and first workers of the plant. The latter was built in three years, at a rapid pace. The construction was an ordeal for some enthusiastic volunteers and for thousands of convict laborers, who starved, were overworked, and froze in overcrowded unheated barracks. But in 1932 the mammoth foundry and steel mill began to function.

Coke was brought to Magnitogorsk from the great Kuznetsk Coal Basin lying 1,250 miles away in Western Siberia, and from Karaganda, in Kazakhstan. (Despite their mineral wealth, the Urals are not very rich in coking coal.) The Urals' iron ore went by return railroad cars to the Kuznetsk Basin where large iron and steel works were set up, too.

The Magnitogorsk and Kuznetsk plants supply most of Siberia with metal needed for its progressing industrialization.

The Urals' southern farm belt is the country of large grain-growing and cattle-breeding State and collective farms; of highly mechanized tractor agriculture. Besides wheat, a great deal of millet and sunflower are grown.

The belt's northeastern Kurgan Province has excellent pastures, and the Kurgan breed of horned cattle rates highly in the Soviet Union. The most agriculturally productive part of the belt is its southern Orenburg Province which also possesses mineral wealth. In particular, in its extreme northwest, important Bugulma oil and gas fields are located.

Orenburg (316,000), founded as a fortress in 1735, is the farming belt's main city and sprawls on a wide, elevated plateau over the Ural River. It has large locomotive and rolling-stock repair yards and various food industries. Orsk has a very large meat-packing plant. It is the center of a principal mining area and the site of a large oil refinery.

Western Siberia. More than four times as large as France, Western Siberia is all lowlands except for its southeastern corner. In its geological past it was a sea bed.

From the icy Kara Sea to the Mongolian People's Republic, Western Siberia is 1,500 miles long, and about 900 miles wide. Its total population is 12,148,000. About 90 percent of them live in some 35 percent of the fertile steppe in the south, along the Trans-Siberian and other railroads. Western Siberia's important mineral resources are also located mainly in the south, as well as its largest cities—Omsk, Novosibirsk, Novokuznetsk, Kemerovo, Tomsk, and Barnaul.

In the north, Western Siberia projects into the Kara Sea with the Yamal and the Ghydansk Peninsulas. Between them the Gulf of the Ob cuts deep inland.

Down to the city of Salekhard the bleak tundra reigns; there are swamps, lakes, dry stretches overgrown with lichens (the reindeer's favorite food); innumerable birds flocking in summer to feed on fish, and the sight of a polar bear drifting on an iceberg. Population is very sparse: one person to about thirty-two square miles.

Many of the inhabitants are native to the region—the broad-faced Nentsy, talking a Samodian (or Samoyed) tongue. They work at trapping (polar fox, ermine, muskrat, wild reindeer), fishing and, above all, reindeer herding. Clad in reindeer fur, traveling in reindeer-drawn sledges and feeding largely on reindeer meat, they live a primitive

life in their windowless tents. The majestic flames of the aurora borealis are for many of them the main source of lighting during the long
Arctic nights.

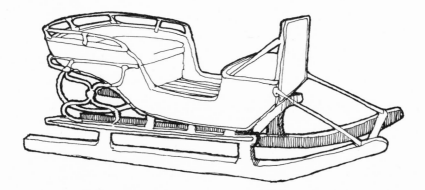

The tundra belt, plus the northern fringe of the taiga, form the
Yamalo-Nenets National District of Western Siberia's northernmost
Tyumen Province. That ND is larger than Texas but numbers only
70,000 people, of whom half are Russians and Ukrainians and less
than half or the remainder are Nentsy. The ND's center is the tiny
Salekhard, sitting at the Ob's estuary. It has vocational schools for
the Nentsy, a fish-canning combine, and a sawmilling plant. Salekhard
is also a river port and transshipping point.

South of the tundra is the taiga. In Western Siberia it forms a belt
700 to 800 miles high. West to east, it crosses some 2,900 miles from
the Urals clear to the Pacific shore. No similar mass of forest exists
anywhere else in the world. In humid areas, Western Siberia's taiga
consists chiefly of silver fir and spruce, mixed with aspen and cedar.
Pine and larch grow chiefly in the dry, sandy places.

Virtually all of Western Siberia is drained by the Ob and the
Irtyish, forming together Russia's largest, and the world's third largest,
river. Some of their tributaries—such as the Ishim, the Tobol, the
Chulym—are themselves large, navigable rivers. In Siberia's taiga,
traversed by no railroads, ships plying the Ob-Irtysh system and the
airplane are the only means of transportation. Navigation season on
the Ob lasts 185 days a year at Novosibirsk and 155 at Salekhard.

The Ob flows in a deep bed: its elevated right bank rises up to
120 feet. Yet due to the country's flatness, the land is very swampy.
In particular, the low watershed between the Ob and Irtysh, where
they flow on a parallel course, is cut up by rivers and dotted with

swamps and lakes. In spring they all expand and fuse into one endless expanse of water called "Vasyuganye," or the "Vasyugan Sea," the Vasyugan being one of the Ob's tributaries.

South of the Yamalo-Nenets National District lies the *Khanty-Mansiysky ND*. It also forms part of the Tyumen Province and is a little smaller than Texas. Of its total population of 230,000, three-quarters are Russians and some Ukranians, and about 15 percent Khants and Mansis. These natives of Siberia speak tongues of the Finno-Ugric linguistic group.

Lumbering is one of their chief pursuits. Fishing and hunting come next. Valuable fur species—the blue fox, the ermine, the sable—are bred on animal farms. There are fewer reindeer than in the tundra: in the taiga the horse serves better. Rye, oats, potatoes, vegetables are grown in the river valleys during the short but hot summer. Khanty-Mansiysk, the ND's capital (built chiefly of log cabins), sits at the confluence of the Irtysh and the Ob.

Recently, large oil and gas deposits have been found in the area. Two railroads under construction will cut into Western Siberia's taiga and link it, via the Urals, to the rest of the Soviet Union. New and modern industrial settlements are popping up here and there.

Tyumen (218,000), the main center of the province in which lie the two ND's mentioned above, is Siberia's oldest city, dating back to 1586. Sitting on the Turá River, it is a leading shipbuilding center for the entire Ob-Irtysh river system and a busy river port. The northern branch of the Trans-Siberian Railroad goes via Tyumen, which gives it an important transshipping position. The city also produces equipment for the lumbering industry and processes raw materials, in particular pelts and leather.

Southeast of Tyumen, emerging from the mixed forest zone, the Trans-Siberian crosses abundant wheat, rye, corn, and potato fields forming part of the black soil belt which passes into Kazakhstan.

This is a relatively densely peopled part of Siberia. Two large cities as well as minor ones are located along the railroad. Omsk (746,000), founded in 1716, is a port on the Irtysh supplying the north with all its need, from potatoes and snowboots to machinery. This is also an oil-refining city and distributor of petroleum products.

Novosibirsk (1,049,000), east of Omsk, was founded in 1893. Siberia's largest, fastest-growing metropolis, it is a great port on the Ob, key airport, and large rail junction.

Especially important is Novosibirsk's industrial role, involved in steel rolling, tin smelting, construction of river vessels, machine tools and electric generators, production of plastics and of drugs.

South of Novosibirsk is Barnaul, the Altai Territory's main city and a key rail junction. Founded in 1738, it is now an industrial center with concerns ranging from a Diesel motor plant to a huge rayon factory.

Novosibirsk and Barnaul form a double gate to the Kuznetsk Coal Basin, or Kuzbas—Western Siberia's real treasure which lies roughly 100 miles east of them.

Stretching about 200 miles north-to-south and 120 miles across, along the Tom (an affluent of the Ob), the Kuzbas is compressed between two northern foothill ridges of the Altay Mountains. It now supplies the Soviet Union with 17 percent of its total coal—and 30 percent of its coking coal—consumption. The Kuzbas area is very densely peopled and crammed with cities, most of them new.

Kemerovo is the main city of the province in which the Kuzbas lies and is, primarily, a coal-mining city. Begun in 1918, it now has a population of 358,000. It produces chemicals based on the coking industry and is a machine-building center. Novokuznetsk (484,000), is the seat of the Kuznetsk Metallurgical Combine—and of an aluminum plant. Anzhero-Sudzhensk, also a new town, produces coal-mining equipment, drugs, and glass. All of the Kuzbas is dotted with hoisting towers at pitheads, coke furnaces, stacks belching smoke and red glow at night, excavators working on road construction, and new coal miners' settlements.

At the Kuzbas' northern edge, in the taiga zone, Tomsk sits on the Tom River. Founded in 1604, it has long been Siberia's metropolis and intellectual center. Its university, medical college, and technical institutes are the oldest and among the best in Siberia.

The southern part of the Kemerovo Province, named Gornaya (Mountainous) Shoria, contains gold and large deposits of very high-grade iron ore. Northwest of Novokuznetsk, polymetallic ores and rare metals are mined.

The Altay Mountains rise in Western Siberia's southeastern corner, passing from Eastern Kazakhstan and from Siberia into China (Sinki-ang) and Mongolia. Though not very high, their southern summits are covered with eternal snow. Mt. Belukha (altitude 14,600 feet) is the highest of them.

In their woods of larch, spruce, cedar, and birch, there is much lumbering. Roaming freely on these mountains are bears, sables, red wolves, *marals* (Siberian stags), and, higher up, mountain goats and snow leopards. In the valleys are fields of wheat and cattle. On the mountainsides above the Biya River are gold fields, and mercury is mined.

Where the Biya and the Katun rivers meet, the Ob is born. The city of Biysk (176,000) is located at that spot, overlooking the picturesque countryside. Food- and wood-processing industries are important here, for the Biya brings to it much timber from the Altay slopes.

The area south of Biysk forms the *Mountainous Altay AD*. Of its 170,000 inhabitants, 75 percent are Russians, and the rest Altayans. They speak a Turkic tongue and are also called Altay Tartars. Horse, spotted deer, *maral*, and Angora sheep breeding and hunting remain their main pursuits. Their AD's economic and cultural center is the little Gorno-Altaysk.

Eastern Siberia, nearly three times as large as Western Siberia, has only 7,883,000 inhabitants, a little more than half the population of the latter.

Siberia's two parts are, of course, alike. Both have a tundra belt, widening (north-to-south) as one moves eastward; both have the "green ocean" of taiga, which in Eastern Siberia is twice as wide as in the west; and they each have great rivers flowing into the Arctic Ocean's seas. Eastern Siberia's greatest rivers are the Yenisey, 2,400 miles long, and the Lena, 3,115 miles long, and up to six miles wide.

Yet in some respects Siberia's two parts greatly differ.

Western Siberia is nearly all lowlands, much of it swamp; the Eastern part is mountainious except for the tundra and river valleys.

The immense space between the Yenisey and Lena rivers is taken up by the Central Siberian Plateau, swelling here and there into ridges of hills. Its average altitude is about 1,970 feet. The plateau was formed by the breaking up of the earth's crust. Masses of volcanic strata flowed out, and they covered thousands of square miles. Some rivers have cut canyons through them with almost vertical walls.

East of the Lena and in the south, mountain ranges frame the Central Plateau, tilting it toward the Arctic. Following the Lena's curving course, the Verkhoyansk Range rises up to 8,200 feet high; farther east the Cherksy Range reaches 9,843 feet. The crests of these ranges are rocky and sheer.

In the south are also the Sayan Mountains (up to 11,450 feet) as well as the Yablonov and the Stanovoy Ranges (the latter reaching 8,200 feet). In some of these ranges patches of snow stay all through the summer.

The Central Plateau is dry. Hence, the eastern taiga consists chiefly of pine and larch, which prefer dry soil. Trees are taller and more widely spaced than in the dark, marshy spruce and fir forests of Western Siberia. Sunshine goes easily through their crowns.

Western Siberia is cold, but Eastern Siberia is very much colder. It has the coldest winters in the entire Northern Hemisphere, for about one-quarter of it lies north of the Arctic Circle. Throughout most of the land the mercury stays below freezing point for over 180 days a year. In the south of the region frosts occur even at the end of May. The little city of Verkhoyansk, just north of the Arctic Circle, is known as the world's "Cold Pole." Its January temperature averages $-57.1°$ F., and on some days the mercury sinks to $-84°$ F. During these frosts the weather remains bright, sunny, and windless, and the air is crystal clear. Although short, the summers are hot. In Irkutsk the July temperature averages $64.4°$ F.

Much of the country is underlain by permafrost: during the short summer only the top layer of soil (1½ to 6 feet thick) thaws; underneath, the ground remains frozen. Permafrost does not interfere with agriculture, and within Eastern Siberia's southern belt food and technical cultures are grown. Nor does it interfere with such trees as larch or pine, whose roots do not strike very deep.

However, permafrost is a great obstacle to the construction of some buildings, and especially railroads and water-supply systems.

In Siberia's extreme north fossil ice, remaining from the Ice Age, is sometimes excavated. Up to 50 feet thick, its layers often contain the remains of long extinct animals.

In 1867 a whole mammoth, in an excellent state of preservation, was found embedded in such a block of ice. A large piece of its flesh was sent by Russian scientists to a colleague of theirs in Edinburgh, Scotland. It was cooked, and years later it was remembered by one who had tasted it, "it was very black and tough."

The land has much unexplored wealth. The coal deposits are immense, but only some of them along the Trans-Siberian are properly worked; huge Arctic deposits have barely been scratched. On the Lena there is oil and natural gas. Some of the country's many gold fields are internationally known and so are the great Mirny diamond mines. Eastern Siberia also contains iron ore, tin, molybdenum, tungsten, nickel, copper, cobalt, polymetals, bauxites, and other deposits.

In Eastern Siberia the bulk of the population lives in the south along the Trans-Siberian and its spur lines, just as it does in the west. Here, too, are most of the cities—from the important Krasnoyarsk, Irkutsk, or Ulan-Udé to the smaller Kansk and Taishet. A wooded black earth steppe is the country's narrow agricultural belt, forming bulges around most cities. Wheat, barley, rye, corn, potatoes, sunflowers, and *makhorka* tobacco are grown.

Only 5 percent of Eastern Siberia is used for agriculture, and only 2 percent is under cultivation. Yet more grain is produced than its population needs. An important place is held by the breeding of cattle, sheep, horses, reindeer, and sledge-dogs.

Of the land's population of 7,883,000, about 7,163,000 are Russians (including Ukrainians and Belorussians), and 720,000 are its original dwellers.

The largest group of these natives are the Buryars, speaking a Mongolian tongue; and the Yakuts, Tuvinian, and Khakasses, speaking Turkic languages. Then there are smaller nationalities—the Evenki of the Tungus-Manchurian group, a few thousand Nentsy, and the same number of Selkups.

Russians live chiefly along the Trans-Siberian, both in farming and industrial areas; also in cities and mining centers scattered elsewhere. West to east, predominantly Russian areas are the large Krasnoyarsk Territory (nearly one-quarter the size of the United States), reaching out from the Kara Sea to the Sayan Mountains; the smaller Irkutsk Province west and north of Lake Baikal; and the Chita Province in the southeast.

The three larger native nationalities—Yakuts, Buryats, and Tuvinians—have Autonomous ASSSR's of their own. Smaller non-Russian nationalities form one autonomous and four national districts within the predominantly Russian territory and provinces. Of course all the nationalities freely mix. Flat-faced, slant-eyed, black-haired Buryats, Yakuts, or Khakasses live and work as shepherds, construction workers, or laboratory technicians in any Russian province or city. Russians are sent as miners, engineers, doctors to Nenets or Tuvinian areas.

Northern Siberia's smaller nationalities were—and most still are—primitive trappers, fishermen, reindeerers, and lumbermen. Larger groups, in particular the Yakuts and Buryats, have always been mainly cattle and horse breeders. A pre-Revolutionary Yakut princeling's wealth was in his herds. Under the influence of Russian settlers they began gradually to turn to farming as well, in the eighteenth century.

Tuvinians and Khakasses have practiced agriculture since earliest times. Now all of these larger peoples have grain-producing collective farms. Yet in most of their districts animal husbandry is still the main pursuit. A growing number of these people are also becoming miners and other industrial workmen, since much of Eastern Siberia's mineral wealth lies in their land.

All these people enjoy cultural autonomy in their national units. Their native tongues are taught in schools; newspapers and books are published in these tongues.

In the southwestern part of the country is Krasnoyarsk (557,000), its largest city, sitting on the Trans-Siberian Railroad. Founded in 1628, it first throve chiefly by gold mining and lumbering. Later, production of dredges for gold fields, sawmilling, woodworking, a large aluminum plant, and chemical and food industries were added to it. The city is also a large port, for it fronts the Yenisey River which is so swift here that ropes are stretched between poles for bathers.

South of Krasnoyarsk, on the northern slopes of the Sayan Mountains, is the *Khakass Autonomous District*. Out of its 460,000 inhabitants, 50,000 are Khakasses or Abakan Tartars. The AD's main city is Abakan (74,000), an iron ore mining center.

Minusinsk, near Abakan, is the first port on the Yenisey River. Beside it lie the Minusinsk Coal Basin (high-grade coal) and the Artemovsk gold mines. The Minusinsk Hollow, sheltered by the Sayans, has a mild climate—melons ripen here—and is an important farming area. To Communists, Minusinsk has a historical meaning: Lenin spent three years near it in exile, from 1897–1900.

South of the Khakass AD, where the Western Sayans slope down to the upper Yenisey's depression, is the *Tuva ASSR*. Formerly the little land had been part of China (Mongolia); it passed under Imperial Russia's protectorate in 1911.

The more than 100,000 Turkic Tuvinians forming half of the republic's population are thriving sheep and cattle breeders, who have lately become settled. Kyzyl, their capital, remains villagelike. Tuva has considerable assets—gold, non-ferrous metals, asbestos, coal.

The Krasnoyarsk Territory's most striking city is Norilsk (127,000), lying in the tundra beyond the Arctic Circle. It is the world's northernmost large city. Despite permafrost, it has tall stone buildings, well paved streets, and factories. Norilsk grew up amidst great copper, nickel, and cobalt mines. Special nearby dairies and hothouses supply it with fresh products and a short railroad links it to Dudinka, its port on the Yenisey.

One hundred and fifty miles south of Dudinka is Igarka, another Arctic port which overlooks the Yenisey. It is a major sawmilling center and ships lumber abroad. The river is very deep and wide here: ocean-going ships come to Igarka during the three-months navigation season on the Northern Sea Route.

The northern two-thirds of the Krasnoyarsk Territory, including the Taimyr Peninsula, has two national districts—the *Dolgano-Nenets, or Taimyr, ND* and, south of it, the *Evenki ND*. Together they form an expanse of tundra and taiga three times as large as France, buried under snows over half the year. Yet this huge area has a population of only 47,000, not counting those who live in Norilsk. The Dolgano-Nenets ND's main center is Dudinka, and the Evenki's is the village of Tura. In the tundra there is much sledge-dog breeding; Evenki women are noted for their art of sewing boots, bags, carpets with fur in intricate patterns.

East of Krasnoyarsk, after passing a number of smaller towns clinging to the Trans-Siberian, one reaches Irkutsk (409,000), the country's second largest and most attractive city.

Irkutsk came into being in 1652. Surrounded by an amphitheater of mountains (the Eastern Sayans), it once overlooked the swift Ankara River, the Yenisey's tributary which flows out of Lake Baikal forty miles to the east. However, in 1958 the large Irkutsk Hydro-electric Power Plant was built below the city. Its dam, nearly 100 feet high, now backs up a "sea" coming up close to the city. Across the water from Irkutsk is its academic city, specializing in the study of the earth's crust, geochemistry, and some other subjects.

Irkutsk builds heavy machinery, especially for gold fields, has a meat-packing combine and various other industries.

Showy nineteenth-century homes of former wealthy Siberian merchants rub shoulders there with samples of the latest Soviet architecture. The city sits at the crossing of ancient roads to Trans-Baikalia, Mongolia, the Lena Basin; also at the crossing of many air routes.

Forty miles northwest of Irkutsk, around its power plant, the trim industrial city of Angarsk was born in 1956, where there had been nothing but taiga. Now it has a population of 179,000 and a refinery processing the oil pipelined in from the Urals.

The Irkutsk power plant is not the only one on the Angara. Downstream, at Bratsk, the river is cut by an immense dam which created the 303-mile-long "Bratsk Sea." The Bratsk Hydroelectric Power Plant rates as the largest in the world and supplies electricity to a very wide area. Bratsk, a tiny fort built in 1631, has 113,000 inhabitants. Its individually designed cottages are scattered among tall pines. The town is attractive and very modern.

Below Bratsk, stretches of rapids render the Angara unnavigable, but two more planned hydroelectric complexes will take care of this problem and will provide an outlet, via the Yenisey, into the Arctic Ocean.

Lake Baikal, which will become part of this waterway, is quite remarkable. Forty miles east of Irkutsk, it lies at an altitude of 1,493 feet, beautifully framed in mountainous, forested shores, with sheer cliffs descending into it, especially in the south. Half as large as Lake Michigan, it is the deepest lake on earth, 5,315 feet, and the largest in the volume of water contained. It freezes from January to May. Three hundred streams and rivers, some navigable, drain into it. But only *one* river—the Angara—flows out of it.

The lake teems with animal life. Over 550 species of fish and other animals, three-quarters of them existing nowhere else, live in its cold, crystal-clear waters. Among its larger animals is the Arctic seal, and its most valued fish is the *ómul,* a variety of salmon. The lake is one of Eastern Siberia's main fishing regions.

Soviet scientists are, however, seriously worried. Recently, a large wood-pulp plant was built on Lake Baikal's southern shore, and other plants of a vast pulp and paper-making complex are to appear nearby. They all will discharge their poisonous waste into the lake.

It is feared, then, that polluted water will eventually destroy Lake Baikal's unique animal life. The scientists doubt that even the largest purification facilities can eliminate the danger. Will any solution be found? That remains to be seen.

North of Lake Baikal, on the upper Lena, oil is mined and to the east are the Bodaibo gold fields, among the richest in Siberia.

The railroad skirts Lake Baikal from the south. Paralleling the lake's rocky shore, the train goes through fifty tunnels. On Baikal's eastern shore is the *Buryat ASSR.* Wide, flat faces and slanting eyes are common there.

Out of the republic's population of 771,000, over 20 percent are Buryats, the majority of the rest are mainly Russians. One hundred and ten thousand Buryats live outside their republic in the national districts in the Irkutsk and Chitá provinces. They are of Turk origin, but were conquered in the thirteenth century by Genghis Khan's Mongols, whose language they eventually adopted. Many of them are devout Lamaists (Buddhists).

Buryatia is one of the Soviet Union's main cattle-raising regions. Horned cattle, sheep, horses, and yaks are reared. Besides, the country is rich in gold, bauxites and other aluminum ores, manganese, tungsten, iron ore, asbestos. Both its mining and manufacturing industries are constantly growing. The republic is among Eastern Siberia's fastest developing regions.

Ulan-Udé (220,000), Buryatia's capital, was founded by Russians in 1668 as a small fort. It soon became a center of Muscovy's trade in tea with China, via Mongolia (which was then part of the Chinese Empire). Framed by a backdrop of mountains, it is a busy river port and railroad junction and is connected by water and rail to Mongolia's capital. Ulan-Udé has the largest locomotive and rolling stock repair shops between European Russia and the Pacific.

North of Ulan-Udé, along the Barguzin River is the Barguzin Sable Reservation. Sables from this region are the best and most valuable of all. Sable trapping, strictly limited elsewhere, is completely forbidden here. The Soviet Government maintains a number of such reservations to build up the number of valuable fur-bearing animals, for their number has been depleted by excessive hunting.

Across the Yablonov Range is Chitá (201,000), the main city of the province of Chitá, which lies at the altitude of 2,624 feet. The wide, mountainous area around it forms the watershed of three river systems. The Barguzin and the Selenga flow west, into Lake Baikal; the Vitim and the Olekma belong to the Arctic Ocean's basin; finally, born out of the confluence of the Shilka and the Argun, is the great Amur, flowing to the Pacific.

In natural resources the Chitá Province is very much like Buryatia. There is lumbering in the north. The prevailing pursuit of the rural population is animal husbandry. Also the area under cultivation is growing, but shortage of rainfall often affects the crops. The province is one of the chief suppliers of gold, tin, non-ferrous and rare metals to the Soviet economy.

Under the tsars some of the cities in Siberia were used as places of exile for political and other offenders. The Soviet Government took over the system and Stalin greatly expanded it. Lumbering in the taiga, digging of new mines, and road construction were done by hundreds of thousands—or even millions—of convict laborers, under extremely harsh conditions. Some of Siberia's present inhabitants are such exiles, their children, or grandchildren who, though liberated, decided to stay on in Siberia.

The largest, least inhabited, and coldest of Russia's regions is the *Yakut ASSR.*

Taking up some 44 percent of Eastern Siberia, it has only 631,000 inhabitants, less than the city of Boston. Forty percent of the republic lies beyond the Arctic Circle. During seven winter months the calm, snow-clad taiga sleeps, immersed in darkness, with the sun showing up at the horizon for an hour or so. Rivers are covered with six and a half feet of ice. Yet, during the short summer, days are hot and hours of sunlight so long that, along some rivers, barley and wheat ripen.

No railroad crosses the immense land; the nearest railroad station lies 250 miles southwest of its border. This is Ust-Kut, on the upper Lena, a shipbuilding center and a large river port. Here a ship can be boarded which, after a voyage of 1,240 miles down the Lena, will land in Yakutsk (92,000), the republic's capital.

Set in Yakutia's Central Depression, the country's main farming area, Yakutsk was founded in 1632 by adventurous Cossack explorers. It still preserves a square tower built of logs, a remnant of their fort. At first, princes of the Yakuts and their neighbors, the Yukaguirs, refused to pay the Tsar's tax exacted in sable and other furs by Muscovite officials. There was fighting. Eventually they bowed to Muscovite sovereignty and Yakutsk became the Lena River region's administrative center.

In the early 1900's Yakutsk was just a fur-trading center with a population of 7,000. Yet large-scale gold mining, the discovery of great diamond deposits and of tin, as well as the exile to Yakutia of convict laborers, greatly accelerated the city's growth. Now it has sawmilling, food, and mechanical-repair industries.

Out of Yakutia's 631,000 inhabitants, one-third are Yakuts and as many are Russians. The remainder belong to various other nationalities, including small groups of Siberians such as the Evenki, the Chukchis, the Yukaguirs. The latter two peoples live in the low, flat tundra between the Indiguirka and the Kolyma rivers. Their territory is full of numberless small lakes teeming with fish, and these natives are mainly fishermen.

Three-quarters of Yakutia's population—the majority of both Yakuts and Russians—as well as most of its livestock and farms are concentrated in the narrow band of Yakutia's Central Depression, along the middle Lena and its central tributaries.

Once the Yakuts lived much farther south. Probably in the thirteenth century they were pushed away to the north by the Buryats. In their new country they preserved their Turkic tongue, mixed with some Mongolian words. Originally Shamanists in belief, they were Christianized by the Russians.

The Russians taught them agricultural methods, but animal husbandry still predominates among the Yakuts. They lived in poverty, eating bread mixed with sawdust, and spent the freezing winters together with their cattle in tents of clay-covered vertical logs. Yakutia's present industrial development has undoubtedly improved the farmer's situation. Now they live in collective farms; on some of them, farmers have warm houses with wooden floors and there are separate cowsheds and stables. Yakuts eat horse flesh by preference; and, like Bashkirs or Kalmyks, they drink *kumýss*.

Reindeers are kept all over the country. Hunting is also important, especially in the north, where it is the people's main pursuit. Yakutia still accounts for one-fifth of the Soviet Union's entire supply of pelts, especially squirrel and polar fox skins. Nearly all collective farms include fur-bearing animals in their livestock.

Besides pelts, diamonds, gold, tin, and mica, Yakutia produces coal. Coal for local needs is extracted chiefly near Yakutsk. The mining of coal begun in the land's unlimited Arctic reserves may yield great results. At the Viliuy River's estuary large deposits of natural gas have been found. Yakutia's endless larch taiga is also invaluable. Larch is very hard, does not rot, and replaces iron in some structures. Yet it is difficult to transport for being very heavy, it cannot be floated.

Since there are no railroads in this immense land, 90 percent of the transportation is by river. The 3,115-mile-long Lena with some one thousand tributaries is the most important one. On the Laptev Sea shore at the Lena's estuary is Tixie, a port and fueling station on the Northern Sea Route. Important, too, are navigable northbound rivers—the Anabar, Yana, Indiguirka, and Kolyma. The navigation season in the Lena's headwaters is 160 days, and in its lower course 120 days a year. The Northern Sea Route stays navigable for three months. Within these periods machinery, grain, consumer and other goods reaching Ust-Kut in the south or Tixie in the north must be delivered to inland points. The few important automobile roads are passable in winter, and Yakutsk has regular airlines to Moscow, Krasnoyarsk, Irkutsk, and Magadan.

Apart from this, only dog- or reindeer-drawn sledge provides communication in winter, when the taiga is snow-clad.

The Far East, equal to nearly 40 percent of the United States, forms the Soviet Union's Pacific borderland. Often narrow, it is very long, reaching from the Arctic Ocean to Korea. The Russian shore washed by the Pacific and its seas—the Bering, the Okhotsk, and the Japan— is 9,600 miles long.

Of the country's 4,907,000 inhabitants, four-fifths are Russians and Ukrainians, and some Jews. Its native nationalities—the Chukchi, the Koryaks, the Itelmens (of the Paleoasiatic group), and the Tungus-Manchurian Evenki— form only 2 percent of the population.

Most people live in the relatively narrow southern belt, along the Trans-Siberian Railroad, the Amur, and the Ussuri rivers, and, along some sections of the shore. The small Maritime Territory, constituting less than 6 percent of the region, has more than one-third (1,607,000) of its population. The Magadan Province in the north, forming one-third of the Far East, has 318,000 inhabitants.

The Far East has considerable mineral assets. There are coal deposits in various areas. Oil has been found in the Kamchatka Peninsula. On Sakhalin Island it is mined. Gold fields, polymetallic ores, iron ore, tin, lead, and tungsten deposits are scattered in different parts of the country.

The Far East's main asset is its Pacific fisheries and especially those in the Okhotsk Sea. The richest in the Soviet Union, the Okhotsk fisheries account for one-third of its entire catch. The main species are salmon, herring, cod, flounder, and the internationally known Kamchatka crabs, reaching the size of a washtub. At the port of Nikolaevsk, the salmon enter the Amur's estuary at spawning time in such masses that they can be caught by hand. Sea animals caught are the whale, the seal, the walrus. Far Eastern shores, dotted with fishermen's settlements, live by fishing.

The Far East is mountainous. Some of its mountains are spurs of the East Siberian ones. Among its own ranges are the Dzhugdzhur Range (maximum altitude 6,500 feet) framing part of the Okhotsk Sea shore; the Sikhote-Alin Range (to 6,880 feet) filling the Maritime Territory and descending in sheer cliffs to the Japan Sea.

Except for its north, the country lies in the monsoon zone. In winter, Eastern Siberia's icy air rolling down the mountains keeps the Pacific's milder air away from its shores. Very cold, dry winters with little snow (as in Eastern Siberia) are the general rule. Permafrost reaches south below 50° N. Even in Vladivostok, lying at the same parallel as Sukhumi on Georgia's subtropical Black Sea shore, the average January temperature (6.5° F.) is the same as in European Russia's subarctic Archangel. And that is despite the fact that Vladivostok is washed by the warm Japan—not the icy Okhotsk—Sea.

In summer the monsoon blows from the Pacific, filling the Far East with lukewarm, humid air, dense fogs, profuse rainfall. Half the yearly precipitation of 40 inches comes in the Maritime Territory in July. Rivers overflow, as they do elsewhere in spring, causing floods which sometimes ruin the harvest. The fall is magnificent—sunny, balmy—but occasional typhoons hit the shore with savage violence.

In Vladivostok, the average July temperature is 64.4° F. The Okhotsk shores are colder, but the type of climate is the same.

The country's typical feature is its wealth of meadows. In particular, in Kamchatka, or on Sakhalin Island, grass, fed by abundant moisture, grows two to three yards high.

The Far East is rich in forests. They cover half of the Amur Province and three-quarters of the Maritime Territory. Consequently the timber industry is an important one. In the central belt of the country —upper Khabarovsk Territory in particular—it is the northern taiga of spruce, fir, larch. South of 50° N., especially in the Maritime Territory, it gives place to "Manchurian type" forests, remarkable for their variety of species (up to 150) and mixture of northern and subtropical vegetation. Spruce, larch, Manchurian cedar with a lovely crown of blue needles, rub shoulders with oaks, maples, elms, cork trees, and the Amur lilac which attains the size of an apple tree. Many of them are entwined by lianas; underfoot there are giant ferns and grass.

Varied, too, is the region's animal kingdom. Dwellers of the northern taiga, or even tundra—the brown bear, the sable, the wolverine, the reindeer—coexist in the Maritime Territory with the southern spotted deer, the tiger, the Himalayan bear.

The Far East's main farming area is the Zeya-Bureyan Plain, some 400 miles long by 200-odd wide, framed by the Amur and its navigable tributaries, the Zeya and the Bureya. It yields 65 percent of the country's home-grown wheat, corn, rye (in which the country is not self-sufficient). The area's main center is Blagoveschensk, on the Amur, processing the local farm produce. Another important farming area is near Vladivostok, around Lake Khanka, and along the Ussuri River, confining the Maritime Province from the east. Rice, sugar beets, soy beans, wheat, and a great deal of potatoes are planted here.

The Amur, one of Russia's greatest rivers, is a very important transportation artery, and serves as a frontier between the Far East and China. Only in the southeastern corner of the country does that role pass to the Ussuri, its main tributary.

Khabarovsk (420,000) is not only the main city of its Territory, but also the Far East's largest metropolis, its military headquarters and its main industrial, cultural, and transportation center. It was founded in 1858. Its industries are machine-building, oil (chiefly Sakhalin oil) refining, and food processing.

It sits on the Amur and on the Trans-Siberian Railroad, where the latter crosses the river over a long and spectacular bridge. Khabarovsk has a busy airport and river port. The river, very wide and majestic here, is alive with darting fishing boats, steamers, oil barges, tugs towing long "cigars" (lumber rafts).

West of Khabarovsk is the *Jewish Autonomous District* with its little capital, Birobidzhan (44,000), on the Trans-Siberian.

There are about 3 million Jews in the Soviet Union; they live in all of its regions and engage in all occupations. The Jewish AD was formed in 1934 for Jewish city dwellers wishing to become farmers. It lies in the fertile Amur valley; its foothill area contains iron and tin ores, sandstone, marble.

The Jewish AD has 173,000 inhabitants, of whom 78 percent are Russians, 9 percent Jews and as many Ukrainians. It has large collective farms. Farm machinery, furniture, paper, and some other industries have grown in it.

North of Khabarovsk, also on the Amur, is Komsomolsk. It owes its name to *komsomoltsy*, or members of the Union of Communist Youths who, answering in 1932 the Communist Party's call, greatly helped to build it from scratch. Now it has 207,000 inhabitants. Its Amurstal plant is very important for it is the only steel plant in the Far East.

The main Soviet Pacific port and second-largest Far Eastern city (379,000) is Vladivostok, often referred to as "the Russian San Francisco." From a rocky peninsula which juts out into the Peter the Great Bay of the Japan Sea, Vladivostok descends, in a steep amphitheater, to an arm of that bay called the Golden Horn. Framed by pointed, treeless summits and by meadows with bright flowers, the city is very picturesque.

It is the main Soviet naval base in the Pacific, and it is believed that important sites for the development of ballistic missiles are around it. It is a well-equipped commercial port with a forest of cranes rising over storehouses and refrigeration plants. It is a base of Soviet whaling and fishing trawlers' fleets. Vladivostok's chief industries—ship repairing, machine-building, fish processing and canning—are related to its functions as a port.

Since 1955, in the nearby America Bay, Nakhodka, another Soviet port, has grown up. The Sikhote-Alin Mountains drop steeply 1,500 feet into the sea beside it. It has considerably unburdened the overburdened Vladivostok.

The Trans-Siberian emerges on Russia's "Pacific waterfront." But no railroad (except for a tiny one) parallels that endless "waterfront." Boats, airplanes, and sledges are the main means of transportation. Proceeding from south to north, the main elements of that world are:

Sakhalin Island, 600 miles long, but no wider than 90 miles. The narrow Tartary Strait separates it from the mainland. Its north is washed by the cold Okhotsk, the south by the warm Japan Sea. The conflict of the two climates causes especially high moisture and frequent fogs. Sakhalin's north is low, swampy; the rest is mountainous and forested. In the south, winters are snowy and mild; there are large bamboo thickets. Sakhalin's population (600,000) is predominantly Russian, with a small percentage of Paleoasiatic Nivkhi (or Golyaks) and Tungus Orochi.

In 1905, after an unsuccessful war, Russia lost Sakhalin's southern half to Japan. After World War II the Soviets recovered the loss—and gained the Kuril Islands besides. This has made of the Okhotsk Sea a virtually closed Soviet sea.

Oil is extracted in northern Sakhalin; coal is mined in its center and south. Timbering and pulp-and-paper industry play a role. All along the shore there are fishing and canning, which is also true of the Kurils forming part of Sakhalin Province. Sakhalin's neat capital, near its southern shore, is Novo-Sakhalinsk (90,000), linked by rail to the center of the island.

The Kamchatka Province, including the peninsula, an area north of it, and the Commander Islands (with seal rookeries), is almost as large as France. Except for the shore with fishing settlements and canning factories, and Petropavlovsk (119,000), its capital, the land is little inhabited.

The isthmus leading to the mainland is low-lying tundra, but the peninsula is wooded and mountainous. Its two main ranges are the highest in the Far East. They contain a hundred conic, pointed volcanos, called *sopki*, many of them snow-covered and a number of them are active. Mt. Klyuchevskaye, the highest of them, (15,600 feet), erupted thirty times in 230 years. The peninsula's main river is Kamchatka River. Geologically, the volcanic Kuril Islands are an obvious semi-submerged continuation of Kamchatka's volcanic range.

Kamchatka's fishermen have competitors—the bears, in which the peninsula is very rich and whose favorite diet is fish. Next in importance to fishing and canning comes hunting: Kamchatka accounts for 75 percent of the Far East's pelts.

The northern part of the Kamchatka Province forms the large *Koryak National District*. Of its population of 37,000, about 4,000 are Koryaks, of the Paleoasiatic group. The ND's center, Palana, is no more than a large village.

The Magadan Province, twice as large as France, forms the northeasternmost part of the Soviet Union's territory. It is washed by the East Siberian and the Chukotsk seas of the Arctic Ocean (with a shoreline of about 700 miles), by the Bering Strait separating Russia from America, and by the Bering and Okhotsk seas.

Like some of the Siberian regions, it is a land of long Arctic nights, of temperature going down to $-40°$ F., of bare, rocky mountains and of the tundra occupying the bulk of the province, with only the southern 11 percent of it wooded. It is rich in gold, tin, tungsten, and coal; their mining is now being organized.

Magadan (81,000), the main city, with large buildings and factories, overlooks an Okhotsk Sea bay from a hilly terrain.

The large northeastern part of the province forms the *Chukotsk National District*. Among the native peoples inhabiting it are the Chukchi (over 10,000), Koryaks and Yukaguirs; the Tungus Evens (3,000); some Eskimos and others. Some are still largely nomadic. Ethnographers believe that some of the peoples of Siberia are related to some of the American Indians. These nationalities form, however, a small percentage in the province's population (318,000), which is chiefly Russian. The National District's main city and port is Anadyr, on the river of that name.

The northeastern part of the District lies on the Chukotsk Peninsula. The peninsula's rocky northeasternmost portion, protruding into the Bering Strait, is called Cape Dezhnev. On it is Port Uelen—a port of the Northern Sea Route.

The cape is named for Semyon Dezhnev, a Cossack from Yakutsk, who in 1648, braving icebergs and icy storms, in a primitive boat with a sail made of a hide and a crew of fifteen, sailed from the Kolyma River's estuary eastward. He crossed the East-Siberian and the Chukotsk seas, turned south and passed through what is now known as the Bering Strait and landed, south of it, in the estuary of the Anadyr River, in the Anadyr Bay of the Bering Sea. Four other boats that had been with him perished.

Thus, Dezhnev was the first European to have sailed through the Bering Strait establishing that Siberia and America were two continents separated by a strait, and not one as some believed.

Neither Dezhnev nor the Muscovite authorities who read his report, suspected the real meaning of his discovery. It was seventy-five years before the question whether Asia and America were one continent began to arouse great interest in Europe's scientific circles.

In 1725, three weeks before his death, Peter the Great commissioned Captain Vitus Bering, Danish-born officer of the Russian Navy, to undertake an expedition to supply an answer to that question.

Bering lead two expeditions (1725–1741 and 1733–1741). Sailing northeast from Petropavlovsk (which he had himself founded on Kamchatka), he ascertained that there was a strait between Asia and America. He discovered St. Lawrence Island, sighted Alaska's southern shore, and discovered some of the Aleutian Islands.

As Alaska's discoverers, the Russians colonized it. Their first settlement appeared on Kodiak Island in 1784. From 1799 on, Alaska was governed by the semi-official Russian-American Company, with headquarters in Irkutsk, Eastern Siberia. In 1804, Sitka, capital of Russian America, was founded by Alexander Baranov, talented manager of the Company and Alaska's administrator. Fishing and trapping remained both the natives' and most Russian colonizers' main pursuits. Sitka, with its social life, attracted traders, merchants, seamen, and hunters.

Russian colonies stretched beyond Alaska along the coast as well. Fort Ross, in California, was the southernmost point of their penetration. In 1867, Alaska was sold by the Russian Government to the United States for $7,200,000. Russian settlements farther south had been withdrawn before that.

Even now the Soviet Union and the United States are not separated by as great a distance as it might appear.

In the middle of the 50-mile wide Bering Strait, are two rocky, dome-shaped Diomede Islands, lying about a mile apart. A few Eskimos live on them. The western island belongs to the United States; the eastern to the Soviet Union. On the rare clear days, when the Bering Strait is not enveloped in fog, a Russian can stand on Soviet territory and discern, far away, America's (Alaska's) dim outlines; and an American, standing on his own soil, can see Russia.

INDEX

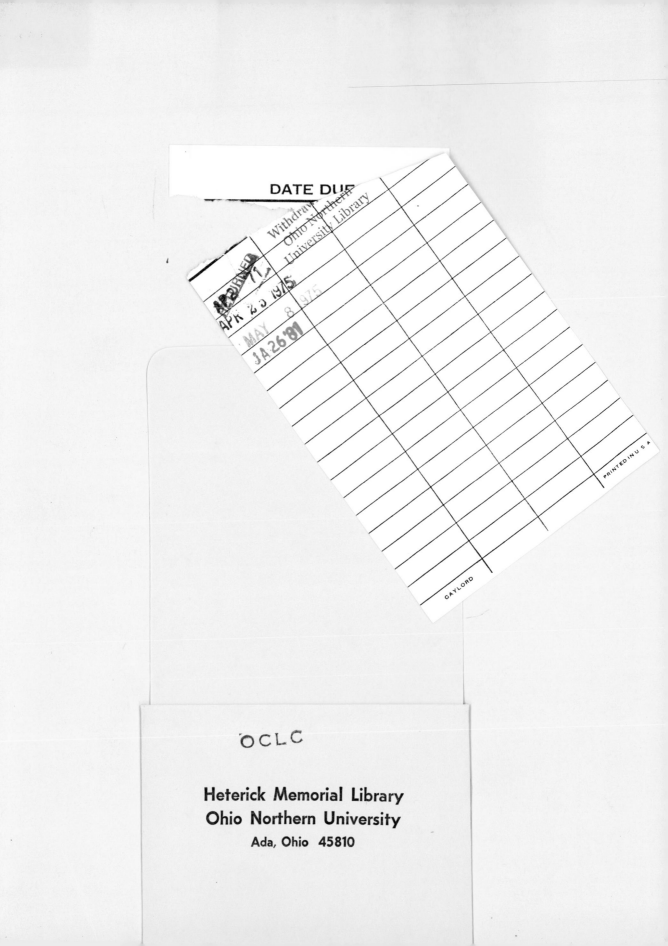

DATE DUE

PRINTED IN U S A

GAYLORD